BOOKS BY JOHN MASON BROWN

The Ordeal of a Playwright:
Robert E. Sherwood and The Challenge of War

The Worlds of Robert E. Sherwood: Mirror to His Times
Dramatis Personae
Through These Men
As They Appear
Daniel Boone: The Opening of the Wilderness
Still Seeing Things
Morning Faces
Seeing More Things
Seeing Things
Many a Watchful Night
To All Hands: An Amphibious Adventure
Insides Out
Accustomed as I Am
Broadway in Review
Two on the Aisle
The Art of Playgoing
Letters from Greenroom Ghosts
The Modern Theatre in Revolt
Upstage

EDITED BY JOHN MASON BROWN

The Ladies' Home Journal Treasury
The Portable Charles Lamb
The American Theatre—1752-1934—as Seen by Its Critics
(with Montrose J. Moses)

Including

THERE SHALL BE NO NIGHT

by

Robert E. Sherwood

THE ORDEAL OF A PLAYWRIGHT

ROBERT E. SHERWOOD
AND THE CHALLENGE OF WAR

by

John Mason Brown

Edited and with an Introduction by Norman Cousins

HARPER & ROW, PUBLISHERS

New York, Evanston, and London

CONTENTS

INTRODUCTION

This book tells the story of a great American play—how it was written, the world crisis that produced it, the profound change it wrought in the life of the author.

The playwright was Robert E. Sherwood; the play, *There Shall Be No Night*. It was written because the rise of predatory totalitarianism in Europe deprived Sherwood of peace—just as it had deprived millions of Europeans of both their peace and their freedom. Sherwood had been brought up—as had most history-conscious young men of his generation—with the notion that the way to avert war was to spurn it. There had been nothing in his education to prepare him for a situation in which war came about not because many men were indifferent to the hell of it but because a few men had the power to unleash it.

The intellectual, emotional, and spiritual upheaval produced by Hitlerism shattered attitudes about war that had taken hold in a large part of the Western world after the First World War. According to this view, wars were fought almost exclusively for economic gain. Hence, just by being alert to the machinations of the merchants of death, people could liberate themselves from mass bloodshed. When Adolph Hitler and Joseph Stalin signed a paper in 1939 which declared that neither would attack the other and which freed them for attacking anyone else, it finally became clear that the same megalomaniacs who could capture control of nations had the power to try to control the world. It was discovered, too, that justice and the good had no claim on the future when left detached and unmanned.

Robert E. Sherwood was not among the first to come to these realizations. What he did do, however, was to put to work the combined force of his dramatic power and his natural sense of human justice in helping to shape public opinion about the implications of the war in Europe.

There Shall Be No Night, therefore, is basically a historic play. It enabled men to change their ideas. The story behind the play is also historic. It provides a sharper and fuller view of the events surrounding World War II than is afforded by most formal records of the period. And since the play deals with the eternal challenge of war, it has enduring value.

How did this account of *There Shall Be No Night* come to be written?

The first volume of John Mason Brown's biography of Robert E. Sherwood appeared in 1965. He was at work on the second and concluding volume when he died in 1969. He left behind a completed section dealing with the intellectual and spiritual ordeal of Robert E. Sherwood in the period culminating in the outbreak of the Second World War. This narrative forms the present volume.

It may be in order at this point to comment on the extent to which John Mason Brown's own life had been connected to and shaped by his decision to write a biography of Robert E. Sherwood.

In one of his lectures, John Mason Brown once spoke of the poignant fate of the writer who commits himself to an idea, then discovers the idea has become his jailor. To illustrate his point, he cited George C. D. Odell, a professor of drama at Columbia University who set about writing a history of the New York stage. He had no way of knowing at the time that the "several" volumes would become fifteen and would preoccupy him for thirty years without the satisfaction of ever completing his project. The additional irony was that the last few volumes of the series took more time to prepare than the number of years they covered.

John Brown's own "magic prison," to borrow a phrase applied much later by Archibald MacLeish to Emily Dickinson, was his biography of Robert E. Sherwood. The reasons for the commitment were clear enough. Everything about the man and his work engaged Brown's imagination. The affinity was deep. Both men had a passionate involvement in the theatre. Both were caught up in the larger drama of the age. Both had a highly developed sense of history; they were mindful of present dangers but also captivated by a vision of a world congenial to the quest for human perfectibility. What Brown especially admired in Sherwood's approach to the theatre was that he did not trifle with people's hopes. He gave them good reason for believing in better things. When Sherwood wrote the story of Roosevelt and Hopkins he manifested the same affirmations about living history that later led John Brown to interrupt his own career to devote himself fully to Sherwood's own life story.

But the life of Sherwood was to lay strong hands on John Brown. Like George Odell, Brown would never again be free. He would never again have an open season in which he could work or not as he wished. The decision to write the biography expended all Brown's other options. The very capaciousness and complexity of Sherwood's life were to dominate his own. For what was intended as a leave of absence from his lecturing, dramatic criticism, and reporter-at-large writing for the *Saturday Review* eventually became a new way of life. It was difficult to imagine John Brown spurning the platform. He was indisputably the nation's number-one speaker. Few lecturers were better loved or spoke before more diverse groups. Few derived more enjoyment from the experience. The fact that Brown gave up the platform for Sherwood is both a tribute to the power of the subject and a testimonial to the vast requirements of the job.

"I suppose I should have known that a man like Sherwood would make notes and keep files, but I had no idea how prodigious the files would be," John Brown told me one month after he began work on Sherwood's life. "I've got a special place where I have gathered all the research materials. The deeper I get into it, the more excited I become."

Also the more captivated. He became so immersed that it seemed to many of his friends that he was living another man's life, constantly and consciously trying to

see new events and ideas as he thought Sherwood might
see them. And the profusion of the research materials
pointed unmistakably to a multivolume undertaking. They
reflected the fact that Sherwood lived two complete professional lives. One was as a playwright, a major figure
in the theatre of his time, whose plays included *Abe
Lincoln in Illinois, The Petrified Forest, Idiot's Delight,
Reunion in Vienna,* and, of course, *There Shall Be No
Night.*

Then there was Sherwood the public citizen, aide and
confidant to the President of the United States during
the greatest ordeal in the nation's history. Sherwood's
history of the war years in Washington tells of the affinity between the minds of Roosevelt and Hopkins. But
those who knew all three men have said that Roosevelt
and Sherwood were no less responsive to each other.

Hopkins was an ideal working partner for Roosevelt.
He understood the President's needs and could carry
out complex assignments requiring full knowledge of the
way Roosevelt would react in a given situation. But not
even Hopkins had Sherwood's gift for penetrating Roosevelt's vision and moral imagination. Philosophically,
Roosevelt and Sherwood were beautifully mated. They
thrilled to the same heroes in American history. Their
sense of human values was in a condition of constant over-
lay. They were animated by the same prospects. Sherwood
had the words; Roosevelt had the instant recognition. This
is not to minimize the central role played by Judge Samuel
Rosenman in the drafting of F.D.R.'s speeches. But Sherwood provided a poetic and historical dimension at a
time when the President had to raise the American people
to new heights in the cause of their survival.

Sherwood was a key figure in creating and carrying out presidential policy in the field of war information. He was deeply involved in the sequence of events leading up to the creation of the Office of War Information under Elmer Davis, his good friend, although the two men did not always agree about the proper role for the government in wartime news operations.

In this volume, then, we find two separate but related themes. One is of the playwright at work on the most demanding theme of his life. It is a sort of anatomy of the creative process, telling of the interaction between agony and ecstasy in bringing a play to birth. The second theme is of the impact of the play on the playwright. It deals with the tension between world events and the turn of a playwright's mind. In this sense, the book tells of one man's education in response to the history of the thirties and early forties.

Sherwood was one of the first writers to perceive that a prime element of uniqueness of the twentieth century was that the consequences of great events suddenly extended to the whole of the human race. He knew that the Second World War was the first such great event. If his thinking about America's role in world affairs changed from what it had been in the early years following the First World War, it was largely because he realized that the whole of the human situation was involved.

He had promised himself as a young man he would never allow himself to be swept away by the rhetoric of war. But, like Franklin D. Roosevelt and Harry Hopkins, he was to discover that his promises were bound up in a set of assumptions that no longer had meaning. For nothing in contemporary education or philosophy had prepared men for the reality of concentration camps, predatory mass attack, or people buried under the rubble of bombed cities. It became impossible for Sherwood to believe in the sustaining power of the old virtues, left unattended and undefended.

The account of Sherwood's disillusion with disillusion and his awakening to what he regarded as the major purpose of his life are the main thrust of this book. It is especially to be recommended to readers under thirty—or even forty—for it provides an interior view of a period in American history that is being subjected today to some of the same kind of scrutiny and appraisal that was so prevalent after the First World War.

What John Mason Brown does not say in his accounts of Robert Sherwood's inner upheaval is that he himself experienced the same ordeal. His commitment to the theatre was no less profound than Sherwood's, although Brown's points of contact were as critic and drama historian. (It should be said that Brown was not without abilities as performer, judging by his highly successful renditions of highlights from the plays he was reviewing on his lecture tours. Brown readily confessed he couldn't resist the opportunity to be a ham under circumstances that shielded him from the judgments of his peers.)

John Mason Brown turned his creativity in many directions, but his main bent was the theatre; he was probably its leading authority and certainly its best friend. For many years he was drama critic of the *Saturday Review*. He was a member of the board of judges of the Book-of-the-Month Club. He had few peers as a writer and none as a public speaker. He was a man of infinite charm and unsurpassed wit. He was as creative and artistic about his friendships as he was about his work.

John Mason Brown was only twenty-nine when he started writing for the New York *Evening Post*. It soon became apparent that he was a critic and writer of prodigious ability. He used words with painstaking artistry and occasionally with devastating effect. He was first of all a man of taste, a presiding fact about his criticism that everyone connected with theatre came to recognize and respect.

John Mason Brown's career on the old *Post* began some four years after Henry Seidel Canby, Amy Loveman, William Rose Benét, and Christopher Morley took their weekly supplement out of that newspaper and launched it as a separate weekly journal called *The Saturday Review of Literature*. I remember hearing Dr. Canby say in 1940, shortly after I came to the magazine, that he knew of no young writer who had greater natural flair for criticism and the essay. One of Dr. Canby's ambitions, which he passed along to me, was to get John Brown to write for the magazine regularly.

The war intervened. Like Sherwood, Brown found a way of putting his dramatic and intellectual talents to work on a larger stage. Here I plagiarize from my brief history of the magazine in *Present Tense*. John was aide to Admiral Alan G. Kirk on the U.S.S. *Augusta*, flagship of the American invasion fleet at Normandy. His natural abilities floated to the top. Admiral Kirk put him to work as a teacher and morale-builder. John lectured regularly to the crew—not just about the life of the theatre but about world affairs, history, and the arts. During the invasion of Normandy, he did a running commentary for the men on board, connecting them to the historical enterprise in which each had a major role. His words enabled the men to penetrate the constricted field of vision imposed by war on the individual warrior. He lifted the men below decks out of their interior limbo and made them integral to the battle.

Some years later Admiral Kirk told me that, for sheer brilliance of observation and ability to convey the essence of an incredibly complex and fast-changing situation, he had never seen the equal of John Mason Brown's dramatic performance at Normandy on June 6, 1944.

Such an evaluation would come as no surprise to anyone who heard John Brown on the public platform. Within a short time after he began his lecturing career he became the most popular speaker in the country, a distinction he retained for more than thirty years. I know of no contemporary critic who used words more adroitly and colorfully. He had complete control of the quintessentials, whether in describing a play, a person, or an event. The pictures he painted in the listener's mind had far greater substance and vitality than those which the eye alone could perceive. John Brown demonstrated that the most potent theatre could be staged within the imagination —without curtains, props, or special lighting effects. And so he went around the country, a composite performance by himself, providing not only drama criticism of a very high order but a versatile sampling of the plays themselves.

John Mason Brown's column for *SR*, "Seeing Things," revealed that his interest in the theatre was exceeded only by his interest in the human drama. He paid his readers the compliment of believing that their concerns were as wide-ranging as his own, their sensitivities no less keen, their feelings no less deep. What he once wrote of Edith Hamilton, for whom he had total admiration, was no less true of himself. He said that Miss Hamilton was "a popularizer but not a vulgarizer, a liaison officer between the finest that has been and the finest that is." She "wrote from the heart as well as the head." Her "learning and living are linked. Large as is her erudition, her vision is larger."

Subsequently, John Mason Brown's writings in the magazine widened progressively until they embraced the world of the creative arts as a whole and the arena of events and ideas. In fact, few writers I know have made more imaginative use of the unique advantages offered by a magazine for combining the public interest in the topical with the critic's interest in the generic and the historical. He would write about Clifford Odets one week, locating him in time, space, and the human condition. The next week he would contribute an essay on a new book about Horace Walpole by Wilmarth Lewis. At one point, he dropped out of the magazine for several weeks in order to gather material for a series of articles on the Nuremberg trials—a series, incidentally, that still stands as one of the best-rounded accounts and appraisals of that event, whether from the standpoint of political or juridical history. I was especially struck with his description of some of the men on trial:

> A sorrier group of men than those who had found their Valhalla in the Nuremberg dock could scarcely be imagined. The prison pallor—that pallor which can reduce the most florid complexion to a whiteness not unlike a fish's belly—was upon them. . . . Their bodies, like their authority, had shriveled.

Only the cruelty in their faces remained undwindled. Inescapable as this was, it was insufficient to encompass their mass crimes. They had lean, though not hungry, looks. It was not so much that they had become thin as that they had ceased to be gross. The change in their diet did not end with a different menu. They were nourished by what they had eaten but starved for that which they had once fed on. Adversity had whittled away their persons no less than their powers.

No assignment undertaken by John Mason Brown used him more fully perhaps than the presidential election campaigns of 1948 and 1952. All the bizarre sounds of the nominating conventions were duly noted—John Brown had not been a student of the theatre for nothing— but he was also able to discern the deep currents underneath the corn. His sense of drama was in balance with his sense of history.

In 1958, John Mason Brown took leave of absence from *SR* to begin work on his study of Sherwood. Sherwood represented the kind of poetic sensitivity and craggy practicality that inevitably made a claim on a mind such as John Brown's. Sherwood's life and energies were interwoven in the texture of living history, but he never lost vital contact with tradition. His unabashed love of America didn't make him insensitive to its imperfections.

It was ten years before the first volume in John Mason Brown's study appeared. During that time, Brown immersed himself fully in the enterprise. The files on Sherwood that he brought together and organized were akin to a major Library of Congress project. He had assembled enough material on Sherwood's involvement with the theatre to account for a half dozen books. But there was even more material on Sherwood's involvement with the nation.

Publication of the first volume, *The Worlds of Robert E. Sherwood: Mirror to His Times,* gave John Brown neither catharsis nor surcease. He was still full of his work and mission, a man in study and motion. His files and research still dominated his life. He subordinated all his other interests to it.

"The more I find out about Sherwood, the more amazed I am about the man," he told me over lunch one day. Brown was still as exuberant, still as magnificently curious about his subject as when he began the biography thirteen years earlier. He resisted all our efforts to lure him back to his dramatic criticism, saying he was determined to complete his Sherwood biography-history. When asked how long that would be, he gave a characteristic answer: "If I keep on finding wonderful new things about Bob Sherwood, I may never finish it."

This sense of perennial discovery was what was most vital and vivid in the man and his work. That and his ability to share it. It kept him youthful to the end. Like Robert E. Sherwood, John Mason Brown lived a full life of the mind.

Norman Cousins

New York City
March, 1970

Part One

THE ORDEAL OF
ROBERT E. SHERWOOD

1

THE BOILING POINT

During the second week of December, 1939, two men, troubled in their different ways by the same problems, sat down and wrote long letters seeking the counsel of the same wise elder in Kansas. The first letter, written on the 11th, was by Robert E. Sherwood, whose *Abe Lincoln in Illinois* had won him his second Pulitzer Prize for Drama that year. The other letter, marked "Personal and Confidential," was dictated on the 14th by the President of the United States. Both letters were addressed to William Allen White, the editor of the Emporia *Gazette,* who was widely known throughout the nation as "the Sage of Emporia." Sherwood at the time was forty-three, Roosevelt fifty-seven, White seventy-one. Each letter was heart-spilling in its trust, and each concerned with America's proper role in the war in Europe which was already in its fourth month.

That these two men, so dissimilar in achievement and position, and both Democrats and New Yorkers, should have turned with their problems to a staunch Republican from the traditionally isolationist Middle West was not so surprising as it may seem. Turning to William Allen White was an American habit. He was the uncommon spokesman for commonsensical Americans who lived in the heart of the country on farms or in small towns. He had known every president since McKinley, and many had sought his guidance. If the prominent consulted him, so did the obscure. With his round face open as a sunflower, blue eyes shining with honesty, and a twangy voice innocent of affectation, he generated this kind of confidence.

Widely read, White had more than learning. He had wisdom. He was a small-town editor with Mark Twain touches who, though as rooted in Emporia as his own newspaper, was wholly at ease anywhere. In his case "anywhere" meant Paris during the First War and the peacemaking, the theatres of Kansas City or Broadway, Emporia's Rotary Club or New York's Century Association, cities up and down the country where national conventions were in tumultuous session, or the quieter deliberations at the Book-of-the-Month Club, of which he was one of the original judges.

Sherwood and White had long been known to each other. Sherwood, a devourer of newspapers, had for years followed White's widely quoted editorials, admiring their soil-sprung pungency and knowing, as Roosevelt knew, that White's thinking was an accurate expression of the feeling of the vast hinterland. Even when he disagreed with him, as he had sharply in the distant days of Al

Smith's presidential candidacy, Sherwood described him as that "sane and civilized Kansan." White, for his part, had been among the thousands who chuckled over *Life* when it was a humorous weekly, and Sherwood served it in the twenties as its movie critic and editor. Since *The Road to Rome,* the older man had followed the younger's emergence as a playwright and, in 1932, after commenting favorably in the *Gazette* on *Reunion in Vienna,* had written him, "You are going stronger every year. I salute you with deep respect and admiration as a lineal descendant of that Mayflower patriot John D. Comer. You are a comer."

Since then, Sherwood had indeed come far. Such plays as *Acropolis, The Petrified Forest, Idiot's Delight,* and *Abe Lincoln* were testaments to this. In December, 1939, however, it was as a man, not a dramatist, that he wrote to White; a man whose pacifist beliefs, long held and publicly expressed, had been shaken by events. Two months before, at White's invitation, he had joined an organization known unbeckoningly as the Non-Partisan Committee for Peace Through the Revision of the Neutrality Law. He thought then that the only way to keep America out of the war was to give the Allies the aid that was denied them by that law. "If the Allies should be defeated," he had wired White, "the next war will follow quickly and it will be fought in this hemisphere. . . . The only sure guarantee against the loss of American life in this war is an early victory for the Allies."

By December, although the Neutrality Act had been amended, the darkening news had driven Sherwood much further in his thinking. Two weeks before, Russia had begun its unprovoked invasion of Finland, following fast upon the gobbling up of Poland by the Nazis and the Soviets. The pattern of menace which loomed larger and larger had become unendurably clear to Sherwood. It had forced him to reach a conclusion he long fought against reaching. He had come to it with pain, and surprised himself by doing so. In his loneliness with his new and strange convictions, he wanted—more truly, needed— the opinion of an outsider. To get it, he reached halfway across America to White, because, "I believe that in our native journalism you represent the truest, lustiest, and most enlightened Americanism—and, for that reason, if this letter deserves an answer, I should like to have it from you."

Sherwood came to the point at once. His reason for writing was "to state the profoundly regretful belief that the time has come when we should intervene actively in foreign affairs, that we should give emphatic military aid to Finland, and Sweden and Norway, and do it now." He added that for this purpose his own "pathetic services" were available. He knew that, in urging the United States to send forces to the defense of Scandinavia, he was asking this country to commit an act of war against Soviet Russia. He realized too that, because of his well-known pacifism, he was exposing himself to the charge of being a turncoat and a warmonger. "But I can't help it," he went on. "I can only say that, as a writer, and as an embittered veteran of the previous World War, I have consistently tried to plead the cause of pacifism and of the highest patriotism to the best of my ability to see and understand these virtues. War is still to me as I tried to describe it in such plays as *Idiot's Delight*. But the terrible truth is that when war comes home to you, you have to fight it; and this war has come home to me."

It had indeed; slowly, inexorably, and with a mounting force that proved irresistible. "The essential fact," he confessed, "is that I can now no longer stand the sight of the present and future world. My conscience tells me, and with a persistence that I cannot ignore, that it is not enough to withdraw ambassadors, to utter noble protests against aggressors and extend tender sympathy to their victims. . . . The Finns are putting up a wonderful fight, and making the Soviet forces look ridiculous; but it is obvious that they can't keep this up for long against such gigantic odds, and that when their resistance has finally collapsed the fierce conquest of Sweden and Norway will follow."

Then he plunged straight into the heart of the questions with which he had been wrestling and to which he could find no satisfactory answers. "You may well ask, 'Why this sudden desire to fight for Scandinavia? Where were you during the rape of Manchuria, Ethiopia, Spain, Austria, Czechoslovakia, Albania, Poland?' I have difficulty giving a good, ethical answer to these questions. I can only reply that it has taken me a long time to reach the boiling point, but I've reached it now. And I have a feeling that this is true also of a considerable number of my countrymen."

Seeking to explain why it had taken him and other Americans so long to reach that boiling point, he wrote, "We could find justification for our reluctance to become excited about Manchuria and Ethiopia, which were too far away and obscure; we could call the Spanish war a local brawl, with bad things to be said for the backers of both factions; Austria, after all, was German—and many of us felt that France should have consented to a peaceful Anschluss long before Hitler; Czechoslovakia was sold down the river by Chamberlain and Daladier—Albania was a musical comedy kingdom—Poland had some of the aspects of a geographical abnormality. In all these cases of shocking aggression, we could find sufficient salve for our consciences—something to be said for both sides.''

Sherwood had been increasingly appalled by each of the previous acts of aggression, but Finland was too much. It was an ''outrage'' that he found intolerable. ''If the Soviet Union gets away with victory in this outburst of gang warfare, then we must admit that civilization is ended and the red hand of the ape rules the world. I believe we must help to stop it, and that by one such localized action we can avert world chaos. If we wait too long—if we kid ourselves by saying 'Gallant little Finland, and Sweden and Norway, though crushed to earth, will rise again'—it will be too late; they will never rise again; they will be dead—and Stalin will be far more powerful, more determined, and so will Hitler, and the Japanese. By standing aside and allowing this to happen, we shall have lost something that is much more important than all the defensive strength provided by our two treasured oceans, and by our army and our navy and our great wealth. We shall have given tacit recognition to the power of murderous brutality—and we ourselves, as Americans, shall be immeasurably the less for it.''

Sherwood had no idea what action we should or even could take. His argument was that ''whereas we couldn't possibly have reached Czechoslovakia or Poland in time to save them, we can get to Scandinavia.'' Furthermore, he was "optimistic enough to believe that such action by the United States would put such hope into the friends of freedom everywhere, and such fear into their enemies, that peace would come quickly." His conviction was that "it is readily within our power to save the human race from complete calamity, and that we should not hesitate any longer to assume our sacred responsibility." He closed with, "I repeat, Mr. White, that I'm speaking only for myself, as one American, and if you have anything to say in reply, I want to hear it."

Sherwood's letter throbbed with the anguish which his conclusions had cost him. Though self-defensive in tone, it was militant in spirit. In Lincoln he had found a hero who, against his will, was at last driven to the point of deciding that the moment comes when appeasement has to end and one must fight for what he believes in. That moment had engulfed Sherwood.

Roosevelt's letter was totally different in mood and manner. It was personal, chatty, and relaxed. Although on White House stationery and written at the summit of responsibilities, it was as informal as if its words had been spoken over a frankfurter on a picnic at Hyde Park. More than being man to man, it was old friend to old friend. Quite properly too, since William Allen White in Sherwood's phrase was one of Roosevelt's "great friends and private counselors." In spite of their political differences, each admired the other. When campaigning in 1936, Roosevelt laughingly told a back platform crowd in Emporia that he appreciated White's support for three-and-a-half years out of every four. The warm intimacy of their relationship was demonstrated by the President when he sent White a photograph of himself in which he happened to be wearing a seersucker suit. In a covering note he wrote, "Here is the seersucker picture, duly inscribed by the sucker to the seer!" It was in this vein that the President began his letter to White in December, 1939, before getting down to the serious subjects that were on his mind.

"Dear Bill: I have had a fairly quiet few weeks with a chance for more thought than during the neutrality bill period and I have been gradually getting to the point where I need a few helpful thoughts from the philosopher of Emporia. That is why I hope that the next time you come East you will come and spend the night at the White House and let me sit you on the sofa after supper and talk over small matters like world problems.

"Here is the thought for you to devote thought to. Taking things in their broadest aspect, the world situation seems to me to be getting rather progressively worse as the weeks go by. No human being, with the best of information, has the slightest idea how this war is going to come out. But, the fact remains that there are four or five possiblities, each leading either to greater chaos or to the kind of a truce which could last for only a very short period.

"As you know, I do not entertain the thought of some of the statesmen of 1918 that the world can make, or we can help the world to achieve, a permanently lasting peace— that is a peace which we would visualize as enduring for a century or more. On the other hand, I do not want this country to take part in a patched up temporizing peace which would blow up in our faces in a year or two."

Roosevelt then turned to the Nazi-Soviet Pact, admitting there were several schools of thought about it.

"One thinks that Germany took hold of the Bear's tail in order to keep England and France out of the war and that Germany today is much concerned over Russia's unexpected policy of action—Eastern Poland, Finland and the possibility of Norway, Sweden, Rumania, Bulgaria, etc." Another school "believes that there is a fairly definite agreement between Russia and Germany for the division of European control and with it the extension of that control to Asia Minor, Persia, Africa and the various British, French, Dutch, Belgian, etc. colonies."

The President admitted that "if the latter is true, and Germany and Russia win the war or force a peace favorable to them, the situation of your civilization and mine is indeed in peril. Our world trade would be at the mercy of the combine and our increasingly better relations with our twenty neighbors to the south would end—unless we were willing to go to war in their behalf against a German-Russian dominated Europe."

What worried Roosevelt most were the Americans who patted themselves on the back every morning, thanking God for the Atlantic and Pacific Oceans, and thanking God too for Roosevelt and Hull because "no matter what happens, they will keep us out of war." He added, "The Lord and you know perfectly well that Roosevelt and Hull fully expect to keep us out of war—but, on the other hand, we are not going around thanking God for allowing us physical safety within our continental limits. Things move with such terrific speed, these days, that it really is essential to us to think in broader terms and, in effect, to warn the American people that they, too, should think of possible ultimate results in Europe and the Far East."

The President concluded his 650-word letter with,

"Therefore, my sage old friend, my problem is to get the American people to think of conceivable consequences without scaring the American people into thinking that they are going to be dragged into this war. Think it over and do come down to Washington soon—any time after January fifth would be grand. I shall have my message and budget out of the way by then."

It was not until two days after Christmas, in other words over two weeks after Sherwood wrote him, that White replied. He wrote from an anguish of his own, the anguish of an old man who hated war, who knew his influence and hesitated to urge youth to a course of action from which the calendar exempted him. "I have tried twice to answer your letter. There is no answer. And here is a curious thing, in deepest confidence: I had a two page letter almost as long as yours from the President along the same lines exactly. Everyone who bothers to think at all straight about this world situation must come to the same conclusion that you and I come."

Whatever White's fears and feelings, however, he could not bring himself to urge America into immediate participation. His age prevented him from doing so, his decency made him reticent. "I am seventy-two years old nearly. What right has an old man to tell youth to go out and lose its life? But on the other hand, why should an old man junk what little wisdom seventy-two years has given him and remain silent amid the terrible portents in the sky today. I am torn between conflicting duties. I am baffled."

He confessed to Sherwood, "Again and again I have read your letter and always I have stood with you in spirit. Always I have been restrained by an old man's fear and doubt when it comes to lifting my voice for war. Of such seeds unhappiness grows and tragedy comes to fruit. I am grateful to you for the letter. I thought once I would send it to the President in answer to his but I feared it would violate your confidence and feared also that it was no answer to his for he raised the same question that you raised."

White ended by saying, "Let me take this occasion to tell you how proud I am of your career, of all that you have done, what you have stood for in this world. You have rowed your weight in the boat, lived up so beautifully to all your opportunities."

Before reaching his final paragraphs, White with a father's pride called Sherwood's attention to the broadcasting his son, W. L. White, was even then doing from beleaguered Finland. "For your sins," said he, "I wish you would listen to my son Bill who has been on the radio from Helsinki for two weeks and is now with the Finnish army." By the time Sherwood received White's letter he did not have to be told about these broadcasts. He had been listening to them with absorption for nearly two weeks, and they were to prove decisive in his thinking and his work. To both the elder and the younger White Sherwood owed much.

2

EVENTS THE BACKDROP FOR A PLAY

When Sherwood heard the younger White's broadcasts from Finland, two years had passed since the writing of *Abe Lincoln in Illinois*. During these, outwardly he continued to live his usual life, a dark-eyed giant hungry for fun but sad-faced even when he was having it. He divided his time between England and America, and when in America between Broadway and Hollywood. He saw his old cronies with as much pleasure as if all of them were still living in the twenties, which a few of them still were. He played the familiar parlor games and croquet and tennis with the same zest, and bet on the races with the same unproductive fidelity. He dined at his favorite restaurants, kept unconventional hours, and went to late parties at which, when warmed up sufficiently inside, he was always ready to sing "The Red, Red Robin."

As was his habit, he worked with the same earnestness

he played with. He labored unstintingly at reading and criticizing such scripts of his fellow dramatists in the Playwrights' Company as Elmer Rice's *Two on an Island* and Maxwell Anderson's *Key Largo,* assisting with the productions, attending rehearsals, and going out of town for tryouts. He faced the responsibilities of his growing prestige by serving both ANTA and the Dramatists' Guild as president. He turned out movie treatments with his customary facility, including the scenario for *Abe Lincoln.* In the public mind he had become a Lincoln man, and the Lincoln who "freed himself" by making the hard choice for war was often his subject, as when he wrote a lead article about Lincoln for the New York *Herald Tribune* and reviewed Sandburg's *The War Years* for the *Times,* or spoke for worthy causes at benefits and on the air. What he did not do was what he wanted to do and knew he should be doing. This was writing a new play.

Sherwood had come to doubt if he would ever write another play. His desire was to write about what was uppermost in his mind and in the minds of most men still free to speak. But reality for him was making its inroads on make-believe. He recognized that no play could hope to compete or even keep up with the daily headlines. He had faced this problem four years before in *Idiot's Delight.* Then war was a dreaded possibility. By December, 1939, it was a catastrophic fact, a "phony war" only to those as yet uninvolved in it or those who, though involved, had not begun to fight it.

As Sherwood's awareness of the threats to peace deepened, his frustrations as a dramatist increased. To his friend Alexander Korda, the film director, he confided that he wished he could escape from the menacing present by writing "a sparkling drawing-room comedy without a suggestion of international calamity or social significance or anything else of immediate importance." Korda's laughing reply was, "Go ahead and write that comedy— and you'll find that international calamity and social significance are right there, in the drawing room."

Korda was right. In the years before the invasion of Poland, Sherwood was not in a mood for comedy nor would the world let him be. Actually, he was not in a mood for playwriting, and for the same reason. In his diaries for 1938 and 1939 the idea for only one new play is mentioned, and it was anything but gay. It came to him in the spring of 1938 when the Sherwoods and Harold and Alice Guinzburg dined together in London, and the Guinzburgs told Sherwood and Madeline "some terrible tales of conditions in Austria," which Guinzburg had just heard while serving in Europe on the American Jewish Committee.

There are some plays that are better never written, and the one Sherwood toyed with was, as he first thought of it, clearly one of these. "Jewish refugees on a boat on the Danube. Escaping from Vienna, they are refused permission to enter Czechoslovakia, Hungary, Rumania. They see a man in white approaching them. He is walking on the water. He too is a refugee." Wisely, Sherwood jettisoned the play in this stained-glass window form almost at once. The suffering of the refugees, however, continued to haunt him. By the next spring he was certain he had found the plot for which he was groping. "I feel that wonderful sense of excitement—a mental orgasm— which means that a new play has really taken form. . . .

Title—*Footsteps on the Danube.* Three acts—first in Vienna, second & third on a river steamboat. Fifteen or twenty characters, including Lynn & Alfred. [It was an old habit of his to identify his central characters with the Lunts.] Two fine parts, I think. But so grim it will be no box-office smash. If I can knock this one out, properly, I shall have done a real service." When he made this entry, the Nazis were marching into Prague. Once again events dwarfed what he was writing. Once again he lost interest in his play.

No wonder. The storm clouds were nearer, the war winds rustling the trees. England knew this and Sherwood, in England from early May to the middle of July in 1939, knew this too. The English, he observed, said "in the event of hostilities," never "if war comes." Whatever the phrase and in spite of the fitful eruptions of hope, Britain was digging in for a war she did not want. There was no dodging this, even in the peace of Surrey, where at Great Enton the Sherwoods watched their roses, delphiniums, and peonies bloom, and their lupines (according to Madeline) begin to act "as if they owned the place."

The visits of such special friends as the Richard Birds and Geoffrey Kerr were limited to a few weekends at which the old games, though played, had lost much of their gaiety. Overhead the roar of English planes on patrol was almost incessant, a counterpoint drowning out laughter and making frivolity somewhat indecent. The parks in London and village greens everywhere were being dug up to make way for trenches and gun emplacements until, in the scarring process, they looked like the

shaftheads of mines. Yet a great calm persisted which
Sherwood thought had about it "the quality of deathly
quiet." The people, he wrote Brooks Atkinson, "seem to
be confident of nothing except that their government will
blunder."

If on arrival he felt secure in this uneasy England, it
was because Britain, as Sherwood smilingly put it, was
then so hidden by rain and wretched weather that he was
certain no enemy planes could find her. Later the weather
cleared into springtime radiance, and target England,
checkered and lovely, lay exposed again. Although there
were days and nights when it seemed that anything might
happen, the stunned, submissive calm remained and the
grim resignation persisted. Only the headwaiters in
London appeared to Sherwood to be "completely depressed," and he took hope because the capacity of the
English for automatic optimism was "wonderful to be-
hold."

To Maxwell Perkins, his friend and editor at Scribner's,
he reported in mid-May, "You ask how the world looks
to one in England, and the answer is 'terribly overcast
and indistinct,' literally and figuratively. The papers here
are so afraid of saying the wrong thing that they don't
say much at all. You have to be an exceptionally skilled
reader-between-the-lines to understand what they are im-
plying. All the people I have met seem certain that war
is inevitable, and whether it comes tonight, next month,
or a year from Saturday, they are morally ready for it. . . .
Last week we and all the others from the English Channel
to the Thames were ordered to turn out all lights for
three hours, testing the country's ability to black itself
from view from the air. . . . There seemed to be not a

tremor when news of Conscription came out. Roosevelt's message to Hitler was evidently accepted here as the word of God; Hitler's reply seemed to have not the slightest effect. There is vastly less theorizing here about the situation in Germany, Poland, Russia or elsewhere than there is everywhere in the U.S. All they know or care is that, unless a miracle occurs, someday, somewhere, somehow Hitler will strike, and then they'll strike back. There are virtually no interpretations of the situation (of the Dorothy Thompson order) in the newspapers to guide public opinion rightly or wrongly. In fact, the press often quotes the U.S. columnists' 'significant statements.' Nothing of consequence comes over the air, but I have heard people say they wait eagerly for the weekly broadcast of comment from New York by Raymond Gram Swing. In other words, you know a lot more about how the world looks from where you are than I do from where I am. All I can tell you is that there's a fearful state of suspension, and how long it will last, only God knows."

This was England, waiting and grimly reconciled, as Sherwood lived with her uncertainties in the late spring and early summer of 1939. When he found himself in Hollywood toward the end of July, he was not only an ocean and a continent away from that England but also moving in a different world. There were plenty of intelligent men and women in the film colony who shared his concern with what was happening. But, except on the radio, news was hard to come by. The New York papers were days late; the Los Angeles press was chiefly given over to local murders, scandals, and movie chitchat. Unreality was what Hollywood fed on and lived by, and Sherwood surrenderd to it almost with gratitude. The sun was relaxing, the sky had no patrolling planes in it, the palms were invitations to laziness, the beaches beckoning, and his health, he reported to his mother, was better than at any time since he started to grow. Even his *tic douloureux* for the moment did not afflict him. On the surface he was happy and at peace no matter how deep was his foreboding about events in Europe.

Sherwood's experience in Hollywood this time was new to him. He had gone to the West Coast to make some revisions in the *Abe Lincoln* script. These were quickly done and, while waiting for the rushes of *Abe* to come from Eugene, Oregon, where parts of the film were being shot, he dashed off in six days a revision of the script for *Rebecca*. Mainly, however, he was free of commitments and enjoying the rest that idleness brought him. He and Madeline were comfortable at the Château Élysée in a duplex apartment. He sunbathed, played his desperate tennis, and danced so much at night clubs that Reginald Gardiner called him "Jitterbug No. 1." He saw old friends, attended movies, and as a lover of the fleshpots had a fine time at his "first really monster Hollywood shindig," given by the Jack Warners at their "palace." The guests included Ann Sheridan, the "Oomph Girl," Errol Flynn, Lily Damita, Joan Bennett, William Powell, the David Selznicks, and "a few hundred more. Supper was served on the terrace under beach umbrellas made of gardenias and other flowers. All the many columns in the house were twined with gardenia ropes." It was very gay and not a little Cecil B. De Mille. Among the last to leave were the Sherwoods, who got home at 8 A.M. "Pretty shameful," was his comment, "but that's Hollywood!"

The escapist pleasures of Sherwood's Hollywood summer were shattered twice in August, first by a bludgeoning personal loss, then by the incredible turn of events in Europe. On the 23rd he learned, with a grief to which outrage was added, of the death of Sidney Howard, his close friend and a co-founder of the Playwrights' Company. The news seemed the more unbelievable because Sherwood had recently been talking to actors on the Coast about *Madame, Will You Walk,* Howard's new play, which was scheduled for production in the fall.

To lose Howard at any time would have been for Sherwood to have his life diminished. To have Howard die as he did, at forty-eight, was to leave Sherwood "so sick and sunk" that work became "a form of somnambulism." At his lovely place in Tyringham, Massachusetts, Howard, who relished farming, had gone, all energy and strength, to the barn to start a tractor. He cranked it, not realizing it was in gear, and the tractor lunged forward, crushing him against the wall. If life offered the solace of logic, if its pattern included the appropriate, if there were justice in its dealings, Howard would not have died in such a fashion. As a pilot in a war, as a fighter for a worthy cause, and with the panache that was part of him—yes. But not in this way, not will-less, snuffed out, squashed with no chance to fight back. With his death something irreplaceable went out of Sherwood, the Playwrights' Company, and the American theatre.

The day after hearing about Howard came the dreaded confirmation of the Nazi-Soviet pact, which had been rumored on August 22. Sherwood had then written, "This is the world's worst day since Munich. . . . All the horrors of the Apocalypse are with us now." Forty-eight hours

41

later, on learning that the pact had actually been signed, he went further. "This looks like the day when war will start." He was wrong by eight days. On September 1 Hitler invaded Poland.

There is no right place in which to hear that war has come. Not for the thinking or for the feeling, not for the remembering or the foreseeing. Even so, there are some places that are less right than others, and it was in one of these that Sherwood chanced to find himself early in the morning of that first of September.

He and Madeline had attended a Heifetz concert in the Hollywood Bowl. Then they went on to the Trocadero, and there, above the music and the noise, he learned that Hitler was delivering a speech declaring war on Poland and that Warsaw and other Polish cities were even then being bombed. "So it has come," he wrote in his diary. "Idiot's Delight. And what a setting in which to receive such sickening news. The dance floor was packed with Joe Schencks and L. B. Mayers and agents dancing La Conga with blonde, fake-breasted cuties. At one ringside table a group were huddled over a little portable radio, listening to a maniac who had just condemned millions of decent, helpless people to death."

The next two days were days of rumors, confusion, and despair. The weather in California was hot and dips in the Pacific offered only momentary escape. In Sherwood's heart, as he rushed to buy newspapers and listened to the radio, there was chill and darkness. His mind reeled back to 1914 when, as a young man of eighteen, just out of Milton Academy, he had been visiting his brother

Arthur in White Salmon, Washington, and had learned that the Germans had invaded Belgium.

The Sherwoods spent the weekend with Myrna Loy and her husband Arthur Hornblow at their place at Portuguese Point on the sea beyond Palos Verde. There, sitting on the beach with three portable radios going at the same time on different stations, they hung on the news. As the hours dragged by and the Nazis pushed into Poland, the question on all sides was what England and France would do. Sherwood, like many another, wondered if they were stalling. Would they "rat on Poland"? Was a second Munich in the offing? He and his friends, all Anglophiles, believed not. They were, however, extremely uneasy because skeptics were predicting with confidence that Poland would be sold out just as Czechoslovakia had been. The tense hours of waiting ended on September 3 when England declared war against Germany, followed within hours by France.

Soon after the outbreak of the First War, Wilson had said, "The United States must be neutral in fact as well as in name. . . . We must be impartial in thought as well as in action, must put a curb upon our sentiments. . . ." On the night of the outbreak of the Second War, Roosevelt went on the air to say, "This nation will remain a neutral nation, but I cannot ask that every American remain neutral in thought as well. Even a neutral has a right to take account of facts. Even a neutral cannot be asked to close his mind or his conscience."

Sherwood did not fail to observe the contrast between Roosevelt's attitude and Wilson's. "Departure A," he noted with relief, "from Wilson's tactics." Much as he loathed war, he had never been a neutral in his thinking. It was not in his nature to close his mind or conscience. He was a passionate man whose feelings were fervent and allegiances muscular. The England he had seen in his youth in the last full days of its imperial pomp and circumstance; the shaken England he had come to during the First War as a member of the Canadian Black Watch, where he had been hospitalized, and had celebrated the Armistice; the England in which he had worked successfully on plays and films and enjoyed gay weekends at Great Enton; the England which a few weeks before he had seen readying herself for what lay ahead—that England he loved as his second home. France he also loved, the France in which he had fought at Vimy Ridge and been gassed and wounded; the France in which he had later taken long walks, dreamed of history, and tasted again and again in spring and summer the delights of Paris and the countryside. Germany was not only another country. It was another matter. On his first visit when the Kaiser was in his heyday, Sherwood disliked the *Hoch*-ing and heel clicking of its gray, goose-stepping militarism. With the rise of Hitler his dislike had grown into hatred.

By September, 1939, he had become convinced that "Hitlerism was as great a menace to the United States as it was to any free country of Europe—that as a force it was far more formidable than most complacent people in the democracies supposed—that England and France, if we failed to help them, might crumble quickly before it and that then we should be helpless to oppose it."

The question was what we could and should do. Remembering how for twenty years he had repeated at the top of his lungs (as he put it) many of the familiar arguments for keeping the United States out of a Second War, challenged the Big Navy enthusiasts, and pleaded for disarmament, Sherwood found himself, now that he saw Ameria's danger, "in a frenzy of uncertainty," so confused that he could not speak up in public with any positive conviction. In the privacy of his diary he was less reticent and more colloquial. The path which led him over the years to his altered convictions was marked by turns he had not anticipated. "The rugged path" he would have called it, falling back on a favorite line from Keats. Rugged, it was. Entry after entry gives proof of this.

Oct. 7, 1937. Things are getting pretty exciting in the newspapers. Comments pro & con on Roosevelt's speech on world affairs, & on the State Dept.'s subsequent statement branding Japan, indicate extraordinary changes of sentiment in this country. As for myself—my pacifism wanes every day. It's astonishing. I'm ready to cheer newsreels of the U.S. Navy steaming out of Pearl Harbor to go & trounce the Japs! I who used to be sickened by the sight of a battleship. But—God knows, you can't go on forebearing forever. The Hitlers, Mussolinis, Jap war lords have outraged and insulted every standard of decency so steadily that it's impossible not to cheer when someone strong stands up & indicates an intention to kick the living shit out of them. How much there is to kick!

Mar. 26, 1938. Today I read a copy of *Life* with pictures of Hitler's occupation of Austria. Deeply distressing. It called Hitler the corporal who went on fighting and eventually won the Great War. Which is horribly true. When I think of the wild celebration of Armistice Day—Victory—and now look at it. In *The Road to Rome* was the line, "Every sacrifice made in the name of war is wasted." English people objected bitterly to that. They had given a million lives between 1914-18. And what did they die for? Hitler—Stalin—Mussolini.

Jan. 17, 1939. Depressed to read of further success for Franco in Spain, and much more depressed by a long article by Ham Armstrong in *Foreign Affairs* on "Armistice at Munich." I thought of an entry I made in the Diary last September when Chamberlain was flying to Munich. I was convinced he was master of the situation and would force Hitler to an honorable settlement. What a grievous bit of wishful thinking! What a degraded day for the human race when the head of the British government had to betray his word of honor, and kiss the ass of a sub-human bully—and then attempt to assume a pose of pious virtue as a savior of the British home, when the whole horrible situation need not have arisen if it had not been for the abysmal stupidity and worse (i.e. class prejudice) of himself and the faction he represented. Well—they'll have to pay a terrible price for Munich, and so will the rest of the world.

May 13, 1939. Finished *Fallen Bastions* (by G. E. R. Gedye, known abroad as *Betrayal in Central Europe*). Gedye's intense emotional involvement in Austria & Czechoslovakia makes him a somewhat unreliable historian. . . . But the fact remains that he has one of the most terrible stories of all time to tell and he tells it with great power & exceptional personal knowledge. The book fills me with such desire for retribution that I can not rest easily until I have done what I can to help bring the unspeakable criminals to justice. I have to write that play *Footsteps on the Danube* & it must be good. I think about it all the time, but something is still not quite right.

Aug. 22, 1939. Report of a non-aggression treaty between the Nazis & Soviet Russia. I think Churchill once spoke of this as "the ultimate calamity." It would certainly be the ultimate humiliation for Chamberlain & his policy. What an incredible series of blunders has led to this! Nature is indeed taking the world away from the intellectuals and giving it back to the apes now.

In spite of the vigor of Sherwood's opinions, in spite of his clear vision of the ultimate menace of Hitlerism to this country and his resolve to start fighting against

American isolationism, he remained silent even when war came and Poland was invaded. Like most others, particularly those disillusioned by the peacemaking that followed the First War and drained it of its victories, he was not prepared as yet to ask for American participation in a Second War.

The Nazi-Soviet pact in August swamped him with despair. When it was followed in September by Russia's moving into Poland to share in the spoils, Sherwood, though more despairing, continued to be silent. In the fashion of many who hoped they were liberals, he had great faith in the Soviet Union as a force for world peace and believed that potentially it was "the mightiest opponent of Fascism." For him the Russian aid to the Spanish Loyalists and the Chinese substantiated this belief. In spite of the Nazi-Soviet treaty, he preferred to think that "Stalin was playing his own shrewd game against Fascism."

With the Russian assault on Finland on November 30, "the last scales of illusion fell." He was convinced then that Stalin's move was only a part of the Hitlerian plan and did not represent the proletarian revolution; far from it, it was a new and immeasurably more virulent form of imperialism. "The Soviet government was playing the old, inhuman game of power politics with the same Machiavellian cynicism which has been Fascism's deadliest weapon against the gullible democracies." To Sherwood it seemed that "the Marxian principles of internationalism were as dead as Lenin. The Soviet warlords cared no more for the fate of the workers in the United States than they had cared for the fate of the workers in France. The sole purpose of their propaganda in the United States, as it had been in France, was to spread confusion and disunion, to weaken American resistance so that we would provide an irresistible temptation to Hitler to continue his conquests westward.''

On the black day when the Russians crossed the Finnish border, Sherwood wrote, ''Today the most sickening news of this weird war. Soviet troops invade Finland with bestial ferocity. Bombings of people as civilized, as progressive, enlightened, peaceful as any on earth. How long can the conscience of the United States remain dormant?'' His conscience, after nearly two weeks of torturing doubts, told him ''no longer.'' Hence his letter to William Allen White with its detailed explanation of the agonies of indecision which preceded its writing.

The attack on Finland made up Sherwood's mind for him. It was one of the two major factors that impelled him to align himself with those willing to fight for their freedom. The other and earlier one was the speeches broadcast in September and October by Colonel Charles A. Lindbergh. When he heard them, Sherwood was convinced, in the heat of the crisis, ''that Hitlerism was already powerfully and persuasively represented in our own midst.''

3

DIARY OF A PLAY

For Sherwood Christmas was always a festival that he turned into a production. It came as the culmination of weeks of planning and shopping. It was the day when, openly and unashamedly, he could become a boy again; better still, a boy able to give presents with the prodigality of a successful man. Christmas, 1939, was no exception. He spent it, as he liked to spend it, with his family and a few friends. Though the party was smaller than in the past, it remained large in its gaiety. The celebration started on Christmas Eve at the Sherwoods' apartment, in which the wreathed windows seemed sealed against the world. The time-honored customs were followed which delighted Sherwood as a traditionalist. The punch was passed, and repassed, to light appropriate candles inside. "The Night Before Christmas" was read. Sherwood's sister Rosamond took to the piano, and songs and carols filled the air as, with much deliberation, the tree was trimmed. Under it were spread mountains of gaily wrapped gifts.

With its continuations the next day, it was such a Christmas as all Christmases should be but as too many were not in 1939. Of this Sherwood was poignantly reminded when, late in the afternoon, he turned on CBS's Christmas roundup. Among those broadcasting was William L. Shirer, who was reporting how a U-boat crew was celebrating the day on a submarine tender in the harbor of Kiel. These young men, recently returned from their missions of death, had a lighted tree and with innocent fervor were singing "Silent Night." The irony of this moved Sherwood "inexpressibly."

The broadcast which touched him most was young Bill White's from Helsinki. White described the Christmas he had just spent with some exhausted Finnish troops in a dugout at the front. Only some scattered machine-gun nests and hurriedly dug trenches separated these men from the Russians a few yards away. Yet in the dugout Christmas had not been forgotten. There were sweaters and socks from home, and special rations. There was even a little tree, "the last Christmas tree," White called it, because it was the last one to face a land where there was no Christmas. Its small red and white candles were not lighted for fear of attracting Soviet bombers. Its other decorations consisted of a cardboard Santa Claus and a few gumdrops wrapped in colored paper. These had been sent by a child who could not understand why her father was not at home and did not want him to miss Christmas entirely. Although the Finns up ahead would not see their presents or the tree until the next day, the conducting officer said they would not mind because "each man knew why he must be there, and what must be done, and not one would wish himself in another place." Two shells from long-range Soviet guns exploded near the studio while White was on the air. He concluded by urging his listeners in America to look once again at their fine trees before turning off the lights. He was confident that they would prize them the more after hearing about this tree in Finland.

When Sherwood heard the broadcast, the butchering of Finland had been going on for nearly four weeks. This barbarism and the incredible resistance of the Finns had already mobilized Sherwood as a man. White's broadcast mobilized him as a playwright. It was the torch that fired his imagination, enabling him to put to his own uses as a dramatist the emotions White had stirred in him. Two days after the broadcast a note in Sherwood's diary reads, *"The Nobel Prize?* About a Finnish physicist and his American wife. *Footsteps on the Danube* in Helsinki." This cryptic entry means little by itself. To Sherwood it meant a lot. His long groping for a war play had come to an end. His mind was clear. It was not the *Danube* play he had been struggling with. Its setting was Finland. Its working title was *Come In, Helsinki,* which was CBS's cue for White's broadcasts. Ultimately it was to be known, and remembered, as *There Shall Be No Night.*

Sherwood's outline fell into place with remarkable speed. On December 28 he wrote,

> *Come In, Helsinki.* Start with broadcast of Nobel Prize winner, 1938. End with broadcast of disaster, 1940.
>
> Scene 1 — Living room. Award. Peace.
>   " 2 — " " . Invasion.

" 3 —   "   " . Farewell.
" 4 — Dugout. Death.
" 5 — Living room. Finis.

Perhaps another transitional scene is needed between 1 & 2.

What Sherwood was planning, and what he wrote, was a war play different from most war plays. In terms of a cultivated Finnish family he told the tragedy of a small nation lying in the path of Nazi-Soviet aggression. His concern was the fortitude and quiet courage of gentle people who meet death willingly for a high purpose; his implication that what happened by the Baltic could happen in this hemisphere. Unlike *What Price Glory?*, *Journey's End,* and many another, his drama was not mired in the mud of trenches. Although in the final version eight of the seventeen characters are killed or about to die, the dead and wounded are unseen. Sherwood's battlefield was the minds and consciences of decent people forced to fight in spite of their hatred of war. Five scenes in the completed play are laid in a living room, another is in a hotel bedroom, and the only one on the front is placed in a schoolhouse rather than in such a dugout as Bill White visited. At one point, in a home warm with hospitality, a Christmas tree is shown, a small one to be sure but as hung with decorations as Sherwood's own, hence unlike the makeshift tree that White described. In such a setting there was no need for tough soldier talk. Though eloquent in stating Sherwood's new convictions, his dialogue is tender and at times gay in his old fashion. The poignancy of what is being lost—and gained—is deepened because of the decency of the people who rise to the challenge that condemns them.

Inescapably, when he began writing, Sherwood made

some changes in his original blueprint. The five scenes became seven. Minor figures—a Polish major, a British sergeant, a group of young Americans, and a Nazi consul general—wrote themselves into the script to speak for needed points of view. The international overtones, including the ultimate threat to the United States of the Nazis as a world power, were chillingly indicated by the German. The central characters altered and grew. But the play's point, illustrated in various ways, remained the same one that Sherwood made in his letter to William Allen White. Perhaps it was most simply phrased by the British sergeant who, on leaving the schoolhouse for certain death, says "Every one of us can find plenty of reasons for *not* fighting, and they are the best reasons in the world. But—the time comes when you've bloody well got to fight—and you might as well go cheerfully."

As first planned, Sherwood sets his introductory scene in Helsinki when Finland seems secure. In it Dr. Kaarlo Valkonen, a Nobel Prize winner in medicine (not physics), is broadcasting to the United States in the company of a CBS correspondent similar to Bill White. The doctor speaks as a neurologist in a world gone mad, offering Hitler and the new German savagery as proofs of this madness. His lament is for the degeneration of man's spirit because of his success in all fields in finding too easy a way out of life's dilemmas.

In the subsequent scenes, a year later, everything is changed. Russia has invaded Finland and Finland is fighting back. Blackout curtains are at the Valkonens' windows, Soviet bombers are in the air, and Soviet ground forces attacking. By the final curtain Dr. Valkonen himself has died at the front as a combatant. His son, a ski trooper, is also dead. His wife, a resilient Yankee from New Bedford, and his old Finnish uncle are awaiting death in their home, to which they are prepared to set fire in order to save it from the approaching Russians. The only link with the future is the Valkonens' pregnant daughter-in-law, who has been sent to the United States to have her child. This link—and the hope, vaguely stated, that man, because he has ceased to find glory in war, may in time reach the point when, as promised in the Book of Revelation, "there shall be no night."

That is the play, first as it outlined itself, then in essence as it finally took form and was produced. Getting it written was something else. Writing is the willful interruption of other interruptions. It is a matter of making time rather than finding it. At the moment, Sherwood was unable to do either. Even more than most, he lived overlapping lives. The chaos of his happy Christmas kept him from his desk. So did the distraction of jobs that had to be done—such as appearing in court for several fruitless days in a lawsuit over the film *The Young Lincoln,* attending a conference on the National Theatre, and helping at the Playwrights' with the production of Rice's *Two on an Island.* As a result, it was not until January 10, the day after his daughter Mary returned to school and thirteen days after he had outlined his play, that he settled down to write it.

As was his habit, he had begun composing it in his mind days before committing it to paper. When he did start, he was so doubtful about the play that he told no one, not even Madeline, what he was working on. If the Lunts, his partners at the Playwrights', or Lawrence

Langner asked him, he put them off by saying he was re-drafting *Acropolis*. Since he frequently was, this proved a satisfying answer.

There were good reasons for Sherwood's misgivings. He knew the danger of his play's dependence on headlines. Though the outcome of the Finnish war was foreseeable when he began, he had no way of telling when it would end. A more serious block was that Sherwood's knowledge of Finland was at best "sketchy." Like all Americans, he identified her as the "decent little democracy" which after the First War was the only country to pay her debts to us. His admiration was profound for the magnificent fight which she, a stouthearted pygmy, was putting up against the giant that was Russia. There his knowledge more or less ended. For further information he depended on talks with Alfred Lunt, who had once visited Helsinki with his stepfather; on daily newspapers; on a "March of Time" documentary; and, above all, on White's broadcasts.

There was other homework to be done. Sherwood was as unfamiliar with the mechanics of transatlantic broadcasting as he was with how a Nobel Prize in medicine might be won. For details about the first he turned to CBS; for the second, to his old friend and physician, Dr. Charles Goodman Taylor, who gave him ideas about Valkonen's work which were "perfect" in supplying the needed philosophical overtones. These problems solved, Sherwood was still plagued by the fear that his play would have no more impact than "another editorial blast against the man-eating shark."

Nonetheless he went to work and, in spite of a week of unavoidable interruptions, finished on January 28 the first longhand draft of the play he had begun on the 10th. On the 31st he started typing a second version, which he completed on the morning of February 10. Within the next two days the Lunts, to whom he had just submitted his script, expressed their enthusiasm for it. By the 14th, having won the endorsement of the Playwrights' and approved Richard Whorf's designs for the settings, he was ready to have the production announced. On March 2 his play was in rehearsal and by April 29, following tryouts in Providence, Boston, Baltimore, and Washington, it opened in New York, three and a half months after he had commenced to write it.

The speed of all this, in terms of writing, acceptance, casting, designing, rehearsal, booking, and planning, was phenomenal. Seldom has a play been readied for its opening with less friction or more expedition. Seldom, it would seem, has one been written with more facility. Once settled down, Sherwood was always a fast worker. He had completed the first draft of *The Road to Rome* in three weeks, of *Reunion in Vienna* in two, of *The Petrified Forest* and *Idiot's Delight* each in four weeks, and of *Abe Lincoln* in some eighteen days. Now in twenty-three days he had finished the first and second drafts of his new play. To judge merely from the dates noted in his diary, he would appear to have written it with his usual ease. The opposite was true. The play, though "hastily written" in point of time, "came harder than any of its predecessors."

At the end of the day when he started his first draft, he thought he had made a good beginning. He had written twenty-one pages and was worried only because he feared the introductory scene was too short and his characters had not taken hold. A few days later he noted in his diary, "I have no previous standards by which to judge this play, but it certainly works out as the God damnedest strangest effort of my life." As he continued to write, he realized increasingly that "the most difficult job of all" was to keep on reminding the audience, without being monotonous, "that there's a war on."

Whatever his misgivings when he dashed off his first draft, he had enough confidence in it to tell Madeline, the Lunts, and the Playwrights' about it. He recognized that "finished" was scarcely the word for this longhand version. He knew his true labors lay ahead, and into these he threw himself when in February Madeline left for a three-week vacation in Jamaica. Although he was miserable without her, he was now alone, free to shut himself in and the world out and to plunge into that productive solitude which the pleasant agony of writing demands. His battle, as he faced his typewriter, was the writer's immemorial struggle to bend his materials to his will. To goad himself on, he set February 10 as his deadline, the day on which the Lunts, at the end of their return engagement in *The Taming of the Shrew*, were to leave for their Wisconsin home at Genesee Depot.

Every woman pities a wife whose husband works at home. Of such wives those married to writers merit the greatest compassion, for writers are apt to be an untidy lot. They seem to feast on disorder as if under the impression that it will tidy up their thinking. Sherwood was glad that Madeline, a housekeeper to whom a speck of dust was anathema and an unemptied ashtray a foe, could not see the chaos he was creating. Bold as a bachelor in her absence, he wrote her a teasing letter, "You would be shocked if you could look into this library at the moment. It's really a gruesome mess. I sit in the striped wing chair near the bathroom door, with a card table before me. I have one of the cushions from the small chintz couch under me. Manuscript is all over the table, and more mss. and books all over the floor, and a lot of things on the coffee table. My coat and necktie are thrown on the brown armchair. . . . My bedroom is a rather horrid sight, also. But no damage is being done. All will be immaculate when you get back."

It was 9:15 P.M. on the day Madeline sailed that Sherwood began his second draft. By midnight, when he wrote the first of the fabulously long letters he managed to get off to Madeline almost daily, he was able to report, "I've done a lot of work. It's going very well, but I'm still mighty fearful that as soon as you say 'The scene is Helsinki, Finland' the audience will be so distracted by their own thoughts that the play will never get them. However, I shall pound it out."

His apprehension grew the next day when, at a meeting of the Playwrights' Company, he told "the boys" about his new play. Their excitement over it, sight unseen, filled him with humility and alarm because he was afraid he was writing a flop. "I find it difficult," he confided to Madeline, "to get them to appreciate the fact that I've written plenty more bad plays than good ones. The thing is that, ever since I learned my lesson from *The Love Nest*, I've quietly buried my monsters instead of having them all produced, like some others I could (but won't) name. If my typing is sloppy, it's because I'm bleary-eyed with sitting before this Goddamned machine. But—to return to the boys—they all seem so certain that this play is an artistic masterpiece and a smash hit that I dread the day when I'll have to show it to them.'' Even so, he went back to pounding, to hasten the day to which he looked forward in spite of his dread.

For the next nine nights—and days—Sherwood devoted himself to adding to the litter in his library. If his self-imprisoning routine had a theme song, it was ''Pound, pound, pound on these keys. I'm not going out at all.'' Except for a few solacing and needed breaks he seldom did. He chose to have his life ''eventless'' because inching forward from scene to scene and speech to speech was each day the event that mattered most to him. Always one to stay up late, he now stayed up later and, unable to sleep, breakfasted earlier than usual. Three in the morning became the new time for stopping, 10:30 A.M. the frequent hour for starting.

Once he was so tired he could hardly get himself undressed for bed, once so done in that he slept in his chair. He was only forty-three, but at the end of a bad day he felt a stab of uncertainty which made him wonder if he was aging. To encourage himself in what he was doing, he turned back to what he had done. In search of a model he read *Reunion in Vienna*. But instead of stimulating him it depressed him because he found it ''so good.'' The question he asked himself was the troubled one many an author has asked when haunted by the fear that he will never write again as he once wrote. It was, ''How could I ever have written as gracefully as that?'' His comment on a talky scene in the earlier version of his new play had been ''Dramatize this, for God's sake!'' Dramatizing the whole script was the task to which he now set himself unremittingly in spite of a downing bout of *tic douloureux.*

He did interlard his diary with echoes of headlines and comments on the few people he saw, and he did seek to enliven his letters with household details, and gossip about John Barrymore's sad, autumnal antics in *My Dear Children* or seeing Walt Disney's new film *Pinocchio* with a party which included Ingrid Bergman. But, naturally, his waking hours and those when he should have been asleep were centered on his play about Finland. For this obsession he at one point apologized to Madeline, saying, "It seems to me that all I put in these letters is what time it is, what I have to eat and drink, and what scene I am on. There's a good reason for this; it's all I know these days (except, of course, how I feel about loving you and missing you—but I put that in too)."

His first and subsequent search was for a title, since he had decided that *Come In, Helsinki* was "too journalese." Like other authors on the same quest, he riffled the pages of Bartlett's, that gold mine of titles and instant erudition. He turned to Shakespeare, Shelley, and the Bible, but could not at first find one that had the proper sound and sense. Among his varying choices were *The Postern Gate, The Knowledge and the Power*, his old favorite *The Rugged Path,* and *The Defense of Man.* When he submitted a script to the Lunts, he switched to *Revelation,* and did not change it publicly from this to *There Shall Be No Night* until after the Providence tryout and just before the Boston opening. These frequent shifts were indications of the difficulties he was having in bringing the content of his play into final focus.

His diary and letters to Madeline logged his struggles

with these difficulties. They were progress reports of a dramatist at work. In them, with no attempts at literary flourishes, he recorded his waverings between elation and discouragement, hope and despair, as he wrote feverishly on, persevering even when exhausted.

Feb. 1, 1940 [to Madeline]. It's now 1:25 A.M. I've been working for pretty nearly four hours, and have just gone out and poured myself a drink of milk and rye. I'm progressing very slowly, because I've never seen anything so inadequate as the writing I did on the first manuscript. I just simply didn't know where I was going. But it's being tremendously improved in this typing process, and tonight I've managed to get the key-note of the play set pretty much to my satisfaction. By "key note" I mean the essential element which, I hope, will make the play something more than just a temporary propaganda piece. . . . I did more work on the play last night—in fact, I was at it until three o'clock. I was called at 10:30 and was impelled to work even during breakfast. I have to confess that I think the idea behind this play is absolutely wonderful. It's another version of *Acropolis*. But I'm so steadily scared that I'm not presenting it right. I had a slick formula for presentation in *The Petrified Forest* and *Idiot's Delight*— and a great, familiar sustaining character in *Abe*—but here I don't know what I've got. I'm wobbling between *Reunion in Vienna* and *The Anatomy of Melancholy*.

Feb. 2 [diary]. Pounding painfully on. Work very slow in progressing, and am worried I may be months on this job. The Finns are still holding the Russians magnificently, but I'm slow.

Feb. 3 [diary]. I've done about 11 hours work today and am wearied but pleased by it. If this play is good, it's wonderful. It is all of my good plays put together . . . I hope it is good. It could be an "influence."

Feb. 4 [to Madeline]. So—it's now 12:25 A.M. I've just finished Scene 3, which represents about 40% of the distance through the play. I had the usual one Dubonnet before dinner and one glass of wine with. I forget what the soup was, as I was listening to news on my portable radio while eating. The meat was roast lamb—very nice—with mint jelly and broccoli. The wine was awful. I haven't been out at all today and I feel powerful lonesome. . . . My output has averaged one typewritten page an hour, which is appalling. But—although I'm tired out—I feel good about it. . . . It is now 3 :30. I have had three beers. I went to work on Scene 4, which is entirely between Lynn and Alfred.

Feb. 5 [to Madeline]. I feel depressed that I get tired so easily working. I've just typed one short scene of five pages—a crucial scene—and now I feel too depleted to go on. That's the way it has been with this play. There's so much trouble in it (I mean, in Finland) that it wears me out in no time at all. I'm good for about one scene a day, and then I just sink back. . . . I have been at it five days and am only half through. . . . Will we [The Playwrights'] ever have another hit? Not from this pen, the way things look. I guess it's up to Behrman, all right. . . . I want to impart some good news : I rewrote the end of Scene 4 and got it just the way I want it (at least, I hope so) with a real up-surge of hope instead of a down-beat of despair. You see—my greatest problem in this play has been due to the fact that although the steely heroism and super-human fortitude of the Finns is awe-inspiring it's apt to get God-damned monotonous. That may be the remark of a Broadway rat—but one has to face the facts. You can't go on all evening pointing out that the Mannerheim Line is another Valley Forge, another Thermopylae. Somebody is bound to say, "So what?" But I got what I think is a fine curtain for Lynn.

Feb. 5 [diary]. Writing to my wife, plus a drink of Scotch, impelled me to try again on the end of Scene 4. I did so, & think I have it. . . . In Scene 4 I wanted Kaarlo to refer to a German friend of his. I looked for a name in the telephone book under restaurants, then in Schnitzler & Hauptmann, finally in *The Magic Mountain* found Ziemssen. Used that name. Now I have the idea that Dr. Ziemssen must come on at the start of Scene 4. Talks to Kaarlo alone. That can be the real turning point of the play.

Feb. 6 [to Madeline]. . . . I didn't go out at all today. I have done a lot of work and made very little progress. I was going back over previous work, doing a lot of rewriting. . . . The dry rot is setting in. . . . This is just a line very late at night (2:23 A.M.) to report that there have been six hours of intensive work and I've finished Scene 5 (a very long scene) and I'm now definitely on the home stretch. Oh, God—darling —I hope it's good, as I've certainly worked on this one. However, if it isn't any good, don't worry, as I'll soon forget it. I used to take failure very much to heart, because work was all that I had in my life. Now—I have so much to live for that there is no major issue involved in anything I may write. But I still hope this is good, as I want to please you. . . . *Next morning.* The stuff I wrote last night looks mighty good this morning—the best of the play so far, I think. . . . I hope I'm rested after this orgy of work before you get back.

That was Tuesday. Four days later an exhausted Sherwood managed—just managed—to meet the Saturday deadline he had set himself. Before this, having begun to hunger for an outside opinion, he sent his first five scenes to be typed professionally and left a copy of these with John Wharton, counsel to the Playwrights' Company. According to his outline for the text at that time, Sherwood had three more scenes to do. He did not attack these until Friday, and then only after he had talked to Wharton, who had read the first five scenes twice. Wharton was "very discouraging." From him Sherwood gathered he had "made an awful mistake in trying to write the play for the Lunts" and that he "ought to start out over again and find another vehicle for the same argument."

The first reaction to his play had been a christening

in ice water, but the Sherwood who left Wharton's apartment, although "mighty blue," was an Emmet in a
"fighting mood." He returned home undaunted, the more
determined to go ahead with his play, to meet his deadline, and, contrary to Wharton's urging, to show the script
to the Lunts before the other playwrights had had a
chance to read it. By 3:00 A.M., when he dragged himself
to bed, he had done two and a half of the three scenes. At
nine Saturday morning he was back at work, writing
"Curtain—The End" at 11:34 A.M. (he even clocked the
minute). At noon, when he rushed the last scenes to the
Hart Stenographic Bureau, he was sick with fatigue but
exultant. "I actually felt nauseated," he wrote Madeline,
"and was afraid for a moment I was going to snap the
cookies (and perhaps also my teeth) right then and there.
Sheer will power triumphed."

At 5:15 that afternoon, having lunched, seen Wharton
again without agreeing with him, and gone by the office
to pick up the typescripts, Sherwood was backstage at the
Alvin, where the Lunts had just concluded a farewell
matinee of their revival of *The Taming of the Shrew*.
After grueling months on the road, they had returned
to New York for a week, during which they raised $25,000
for the Finnish Relief Fund. They were leaving that night
for their home in Wisconsin, where they hoped to get a
needed rest.

Going backstage at the Alvin with a new play for the
Lunts was no new experience for Sherwood. As he reminded them, four years before when they were appearing
in their first production of *The Shrew,* he had taken a
copy of *Idiot's Delight* to them after a matinee in the
same theatre. Now, as he approached their dressing rooms

with several scripts tucked under his arm, he encountered Stark Young, the critic-author, who had done the translation of *The Sea Gull* which the Lunts had used. He too was carrying a manuscript. Both hopefuls were as embarrassed as suitors caught bringing flowers to the same girl. Both were very courtly, each bowing to the other, saying, "After you, my dear fellow." Which dramatist submitted his play first is not recorded, but Sherwood tells that, after he presented his, he was joined backstage by S. N. Behrman, who had come to say goodbye to the Lunts. When he handed Behrman a copy of *Revelation*, as his play was then called, Behrman quipped, "I'll read it, and if it's any good, I'll sign it."

Behrman did find it good. So did Elmer Rice. Both of them, having read it, conferred late that night with Sherwood in Rice's apartment. It was like a session of the Playwrights' Company after an out-of-town opening, at which opinions were aired with the kind of candor that did not hurt because it was backed by professional fellowship and respect. Sherwood emerged from it happy and stimulated by the many good suggestions that were made. The next morning Maxwell Anderson and Harold Freedman, to whom scripts had been sent, were no less enthusiastic when they telephoned. They all admired the writing and disagreed with Wharton. They all thought that Lunt's part needed building up and that the middle scenes were as yet insufficiently dramatic. Behrman and Anderson believed that Sherwood could do the necessary rewriting in a week and that the play, because of its nearness to the news, must be produced at once. Rice and Freedman, on the other hand, felt that Sherwood should take all the time he wanted and that the play would stand on its own merits regardless of what happened in Finland.

Even more encouraging was the word that Lunt sent Sherwood from the train. Miss Fontanne had started reading *Revelation* when she went to bed and had been unable to put it down. She finished it by the time they reached Harrisburg, where at 3:00 A.M. Lunt reported by wire that she was "wild" about the play and wanted to do it "immediately." Sherwood did not hear Lunt's own reaction until Monday.

The evening before, in a "jittery state of fatigue," he had taken the Twentieth Century to Chicago to participate in the radio production of a script on Lincoln and the war years, which he had somehow managed to write between finishing the first version of *Revelation* and starting the second. From his hotel he called Lunt in Wisconsin and was overjoyed to hear that he was as "wild" about the play as Miss Fontanne. Indeed, he liked it so much that he wanted to direct it as well as appear in it and he had already asked Richard Whorf to come to Genesee Depot to discuss the settings. As for Sherwood, he headed there himself as soon as his radio conference was over, dashed back to Chicago the next day for the performance, and returned to Genesee Depot for one night before taking the Century back to New York.

The second visit to the Lunts was a gay one. Sherwood arrived, a stage-door Johnny in Wisconsin, carrying flowers for Miss Fontanne. Whorf's sketches were found "excellent." There was talk of casting. Everyone was excited and happy. Good news can be the best restorative. Sherwood forgot that he was tired, the Lunts that they needed rest. A celebration was in order, and a proper one was held. "Dined too well," noted Sherwood, for once forgetting the menu. "To bed late." But it was worth it. The first big step had been taken. The Lunts had found a play they loved, and Sherwood hitched his wagon to his two favorite stars. All looked forward to the work that lay ahead.

There was plenty of it, all that every truly professional production requires plus that extra effort which the Lunts, as perfectionists, demanded of others and themselves, and Sherwood made as a matter of course. From the Playwrights' and the Lunts he knew that many changes were needed. His own strong conscience as a craftsman told him the same thing. Accordingly, on his return to New York, he at once started rewriting, keeping the same cruel hours as before, adding scenes, rephrasing speeches, and amplifying characters. It was depleting work which was to continue almost until the New York opening. But this time there was a difference. He was no longer working in a vacuum. His play had been accepted and was being rushed into production. Where previously he had at moments been tempted to abandon it, he now, in spite of his exhaustion, felt excited by what he was writing.

In the weeks ahead Sherwood still knew his moments of despondency, such as the one that overtook him when he attended his first rehearsal and found himself "rather depressed as the play needs so much work. Very sloppy. This is the first time I have heard it through or even read through. Awful repetition. Lynn wonderful, & Alfred." Two days later his optimism revived on seeing a run-through. "Alfred is directing it exquisitely. It looks really lovely. The quality of gentle people is being brought out so well—people who love and respect each other."

This optimism grew as, with each day's tinkering, the script improved and the performances deepened into their final shape.

From the start Sherwood's confidence had been complete in Lunt's direction and in Miss Fontanne and Lunt as the Valkonens, Sydney Greenstreet as the rotund Finnish uncle, Richard Whorf as the CBS correspondent, and tense, young Montgomery Clift as the Valkonens' son. By the opening in New York on April 29, he had faith in the play. In every city where it had been tried out— in Providence, Boston, Baltimore, and Washington— *There Shall Be No Night* had triumphed, winning glowing notices and capacity audiences. But New York—would it be the same? As always, there was a possibility that what had fared well out of town would totter to failure on Broadway.

Although outwardly Sherwood seemed calm, inwardly he was in turmoil. "Getting nervous," he noted, "only three days more before the great day." True to form when he was tense and tired, he suffered a severe attack of *tic douloureux,* which he still referred to as "sinus." The night before the Broadway opening, when he was at a Russian Easter party with Madeline at the George Schlees', a second attack came on, causing him to do something which in his diary even he called "quixotic." "I signalled to Madeline what was the trouble & went home. The sinus was quite severe and took a long time to dispel. I was very jittery & felt miserable. Madeline came home about 3:00 & went to bed. I got dressed, packed my bag, went to the Pennsylvania Station, asked what was the next train out, and got a lower berth. I arrived in Washington at 7:45 and caught an 8 o'clock train back to New York, feeling tired but much better.'' It was a unique cure for first night nerves, but there is no record that any other playwright was willing to put it to the test. It worked for Sherwood; it was a measure of his pain as he approached opening night.

Sherwood survived the hours preceding the opening by visiting the Playwrights' office, picking up presents for the Lunts, and taking a nap in the late afternoon. Then, after dining at Voisin, he set out with Madeline for the Alvin, arriving there at the end of the first scene of the second act. At once he felt reassured. Success is electricity, flowing from the stage to auditorium and back again, supercharging the air; failure a tired wind heavy with death. There was no doubting it—the electricity. Success was in the air. The Lunts, who had toured in a repertory that included *The Sea Gull,* were bringing to Sherwood all the subtleties and innuendoes they had mastered from playing Chekhov, and for them Sherwood, as a man of principle outraged by events, had written a propagandist script irresistible in its compassion. The audience was ''wonderfully attentive.'' There was a ''fine ovation'' at the finish, and the Lunts were ''very happy'' because they sensed that what they and the others had hoped to do they had done brilliantly.

After the opening of *There Shall Be No Night,* there was a party at the Barberry Room, the kind of *Who's Who* party to which Sherwood was accustomed. In addition to his family, among those present were the Herbert Bayard Swopes, the Max Gordons, Helen Hayes, the Averell Harrimans, Noel Coward, the Lunts, the J. C. Wilsons, Ruth Gordon, Howard Lindsay and Russel Crouse, the

George Kaufmans, the Harold Guinzburgs, Peggy Pulitzer, Harold Ross, Frank Sullivan, Muriel King, Richard and Dorothy Rodgers, Neysa McMein, Valentina and George Schlee, Gladys Swarthout and Frank Chapman, the Elmer Rices, the John Whartons, Bill Fields, the Vic Samrocks, the Harry Guggenheims, Colonel Bill Donovan, Fredric and Florence March, the Grand Duchess Marie, the Harold Talbotts, and Edna Ferber. They met in the happy mood that a success creates, but even while their congratulations and the champagne flowed, Sherwood was thinking of the papers. He did not see these until about 2:30 in the morning at Bleeck's, where he read the *Times,* the *Tribune,* the *News,* and the *Mirror.* "Last two notices fine—*Tribune* in the main excellent—*Times* fair but disappointing. This last applies to most of the others."

The notices, as a matter of fact, were far better than they seemed to Sherwood when he first read them. At such a moment, with the applause of the first-night audience still echoing in his ears, he was in no mood for critical reservations. And there were reservations which, at that hour when his hope for praise was hungriest, seemed larger than they were. There were complaints about structural weaknesses, the talkiness of the second act, too many characters being introduced toward the end, and the dangers of writing so close to the news. But from the playgoer's point of view, as opposed to the playwright's, the praise for *There Shall Be No Night* came through warm and clear for the Lunts, the production, and for Sherwood.

"It honors the theatre." (Atkinson, *Times.*) "A moving play, thoughtfully written and beautifully played." (Lockridge, *Sun.*) "A masterly work stirringly projected.

... An outstanding contribution, not only to this particular theatre season, but to this particular time in the history of a fumbling world." (Mantle, *News.*) "A play of stature, dignity and high emotion, thoughtful, eloquent and heartfelt." (Watts, *Herald Tribune.*) I, then on the *Post,* was also enthusiastic, warmly so, although I made some carping distinctions between the eternal and the topical in the drama, which irritated Sherwood. Later in an interview he dismissed these as "academic twaddle." He had moved beyond such aesthetic niceties and knew the world had, too. The events of the next two months made me see his point.

The critics had another disappointment in store for Sherwood. When the New York Drama Critics' Circle met to bestow its annual award, it once again failed to choose a play by him. On the seventh ballot eleven of the reviewers voted for Saroyan's *The Time of Your Life,* four for *There Shall Be No Night,* two for Anderson's *Key Largo,* and one for Kaufman and Hart's *The Man Who Came to Dinner.* "This is the third time I have been runner-up for the Critics' prize," he commented. "The next time I have a new play, and they meet, I'm going to advise all to bet me for place." Once again, however, his laurel-gathering history repeated itself. At the end of the next season *There Shall Be No Night,* which had arrived too late to be considered the year before, won him the Pulitzer Prize, his third.

Between the acts at the opening in Washington, Sherwood had met and been embraced by M. Procopé, the Finnish minister, who thanked him for what he was doing for Finland. Later at a very emotional party at the Finnish legation it suddenly dawned on Sherwood that, so far as he knew, he had never met a Finn before. Not that it mattered. He had made Finland's agony his own ever since the Russian invasion and his letter to White. He had done more than that. As he knew he must do, he had made his play a play about imperiled freedom everywhere, instead of a play merely about Finland. This was where its power lay.

Sherwood wrote *There Shall Be No Night* under the shadow of catastrophes which had multiplied appallingly when, toward the middle of September, he finished his long, autobiographical preface for the published play. On March 12 Finland had surrendered to the Russians, a tragedy which shocked Sherwood as a man, though as a dramatist he knew it bettered his play by giving it a finality it would not otherwise have had. Before the New York opening on April 29 the Nazis had swarmed into Denmark and Norway. Thereafter a hurricane of horrors had swept across Europe. Holland, Belgium, and Luxembourg were occupied, the British Expeditionary Force was evacuated from Dunkirk, northern France was overrun, Mussolini attacked southern France, Paris fell, Hitler danced his madman's jig at Compiègne, and the Nazi bombings of London had begun. Yet in Sherwood's preface, as in his play, the fundamental optimism of this often melancholy and despairing man persisted. Like his Harry Van, the hoofer in *Idiot's Delight,* he still believed, in spite of all evidence to the contrary, "that 'Muma,' the three-legged girl, really has got three legs." He admitted he was "rather surprised," considering the circumstances under which *There Shall Be No Night* was written, that it "developed a spirit of optimism along toward the end." But, as he explained, since he was trying to express his own essential faith, he "couldn't very well keep the optimism out."

In the preface he confessed, "I believe every word that Doctor Valkonen utters in the sixth scene. . . . I believe that man, in his new-found consciousness, can find the means of his redemption. . . . We are armed with more bitter experience, more profound knowledge, than any generations that ever were in the history of the world. If we can't use this experience and this knowledge then the human story is really finished and we can go back and achieve forgetfulness and peace in the ooze from which we ascended. . . . The Mannerheim and Maginot Lines have gone. But the individual human spirit still lives and resists in the tortured streets of London." For him the story of the Finns' three months of resistance continued to be "the story of all decent civilized people who choose to stand up and fight for their freedom against the forces of atavistic despotism."

Since September, 1939, when the war was declared in Europe, Sherwood had toyed with the idea of joining up and found it "a conscious strain" to perform his duties with the Playwrights' Company. "The terrible thing," he told himself, "is that I can't escape from the thought that I ought to be doing something." In his December letter to William Allen White he had said he was ready to make his "fragile services" available. Then and in the coming months he thought of going to Montreal and enlisting once again in the Canadian Black Watch. But he acknowledged that his dream of returning to the pattern of the previous war was "only a form of escapism."

Among war's cruelties is the way in which overnight

it shoves youth into maturity and makes the middle-aged old. Sherwood was twice as old as when he went off to the First War. His health was poor. He knew he would be no good at fighting and doubted if he could even stand a watch. It pained him to admit all this and to face the fact that, if he were commissioned in Canada, he could in all probability get only a desk job. He wanted to do something more constructive than that and, if possible, in this country.

He had hoped the writing and production of *There Shall Be No Night* would ease his mind about his "obligation to render service." During the triumphant week in Washington before the Broadway opening, however, his restlessness returned. When people assured him, as many did, that his play was worth at least an army corps to the Allied cause, and said that it would do more good than thousands of planes and the biggest guns, Sherwood, though pleased, found that his conscience was not stilled. He felt that Raymond Clapper was on his side when, in spite of branding *There Shall Be No Night* as "a rank, inflammatory job, pleading for intervention," he saluted it in his syndicated column as "an incident of first rate national meaning" which might have "deep influence" upon America's feeling about the war.

This was the kind of recognition Sherwood had wanted for his play. He *was* an interventionist. He *had* written a propagandist play. And on neither count was he ashamed. He had known all along that, where he had once been berated as a pacifist, he would now be damned as a warmonger. This no longer mattered to him. George Washington at the time of his retirement from the army spoke of the "great theatre of action." It was in this theatre that Sherwood was now impatient to enlist as a writer. Increasingly, he had things to say about the threats to America which he could not say in play form. Getting them said immediately and directly, without the interference of plot and characters, was to become his form of service.

· 4 ·

THE GREAT DEBATE

As important to Sherwood's career as the writing of *There Shall Be No Night* were the interruptions that delayed him in getting it done. Among these *Abe Lincoln in Illinois* played its continuing part, this time by its release as a motion picture. So did Eleanor Roosevelt. So did Harry Hopkins. And so did the widening spread of Sherwood's interests.

An envelope with THE WHITE HOUSE printed clear and simple in its upper left-hand corner never comes as just an ordinary letter. It seems brushed by history, however faintly. The Sherwoods were properly "thrilled" when on January 9, 1940, they received a note from Mrs. Roosevelt. It was not the first time that Sherwood had heard from her. A little more than a year before, after the Washington opening of *Abe Lincoln* as a play, she had written him in longhand a warm letter of appreciation. Naturally this had pleased him, but now he had reason to be even more pleased. Her letter was an invitation to him and Madeline for dinner at the White House on the twenty-first before a special showing of the *Abe Lincoln* film, which was to open in Washington the next night. Sherwood, whose respect for her was ardent, had first met Mrs. Roosevelt early in December at a fund-raising dinner in New York for an organization called the Open Road. She had been the reason for the Sherwoods' going. "We were honored to meet and listen to that wonderful woman," he wrote. "She is far more attractive looking than her photographs suggest. She is penetrating and humorous and modest. I wish that she & Queen Mary could get together for a good talk about things in general."

Although he had heard Roosevelt speak some years before at a Harvard Club dinner in New York and been taken through the White House twice in 1938, Sherwood had never met the President until the showing of the *Abe Lincoln* film. The meeting meant much to him and was to mean more, though what it meant no one could guess from his diary. The entry reads: "*Jan. 21, 1940.* Washington— Dined tonight at the White House. Sat next to Mrs. Roosevelt, Madeline next to the President. For dinner— scrambled eggs & sausages, cold meats, salad, lousy white wine (probably Californian). The Masseys, the Gordons, the Goetzes, Ruth Gordon, Moss Hart, a lot of others present. Picture of *Abe* run off after dinner in hall on second floor. Mrs. R. said that some representatives of the Virginia hunting set had been brought there by Franklin D. Jr. to see *Gone With the Wind* and after they left she said to the President, 'People like that make me feel like turning Communist,' and he said 'Me too.' He (the President) said he'd like to have the text of the Debate speeches to read over the radio. All evidently like the picture enormously, & it deserves to be liked. John Cromwell there, too & he certainly deserves honors. I liked it much better the second time & a title has been inserted at my suggestion which helps a lot.''

This is the meager all. A hint, only a hint, of characterization is given in the Roosevelts' reaction to the young members of the Virginia riding set. The menu carefully recorded is as revealing about Sherwood's interest in food as it is about Mrs. Roosevelt's indifference to it. But the entry is only the outline of a scene which is left undramatized and unset. Such details, remembered years later by some of those present, as assembling in the Blue Room for sherry, the presentation to the President who was already seated at the table in the State Dining Room, the appearance of the long hall on the second floor where the film was shown, the President's reactions while watching it, his tributes afterward in the Oval Study to those who made it—all these are missing in Sherwood's immediate report. Also missing is any indication of the pleasure he felt, first, as a hero-hungry man in being in the same room with a President who was rapidly becoming his hero, and then as a playwright in having *Abe,* his *Abe,* seen by F.D.R. at the White House.

How deep his feeling was is made clear by his diary the next day. That morning he went to see his new friend Harry Hopkins, who was recovering from a serious illness and was confined to his small house in Georgetown. When he heard from Hopkins that F.D.R. would almost certainly run for a third term, Sherwood at once said he would like to volunteer his services to the President and Hopkins replied that he thought they would be accepted. Early that afternoon Sherwood took the train to New York to throw himself once again into getting the first and second versions of *There Shall Be No Night* written and seeing the play through rehearsal into production.

Three days after his return he sent a letter of thanks to the President, enclosing a transcript of the two Lincoln-Douglas debate speeches which he had requested. "For the purposes of the screen," Sherwood explained, "these speeches had to be cut down considerably, so I am venturing to send also a copy of the published text of the play itself. You might be interested to read the speeches as they are given on the stage. They include some of Lincoln's views on the sanctity of the Supreme Court. Also, in the book, are notes on the source material of the play, intended to assure the reader that I have not distorted Lincoln's opinions to make them sound applicable to present problems. (You, sir, know better than anyone else just how 'timely' those opinions are.) I saw Harry Hopkins and told him that I wish with all my heart to offer my services, for whatever they're worth, to you in this crucial year and to the cause which is yours as surely as it was Lincoln's." Sherwood's inscription to Roosevelt read, "With the profound admiration of one who hopes to have the privilege of voting for him again." Sherwood was a committed man and happy in his commitment, though what his services might be was neither indicated by Hopkins nor anticipated by him.

That was in January, 1940, three months before *There Shall Be No Night* opened in New York. They were wearying months for Sherwood during which he was too occupied to surrender to fatigue. Once their sustaining excitement was over and the play launched, he found himself tired to the marrow of his long bones. As always when exhausted, he was assailed by *tic,* which made him feel as if someone were riveting in his head and left him limp and wretched. He had been seized by *tic* often in the past, but these attacks were the worst he had had and the first, by his own confession, which ever got beyond him. They came without warning and with paralyzing violence and then, after blessed respites, came again. One seizure which struck him at ten in the evening lasted until the next noon. Once he was in such bad shape that his doctor was called in three times in one day to give him injections.

If the *tic* was too much with Sherwood, so was the world. "Every evening," he wrote Behrman late in May, "Madeline and I sit home—I with a black bandage over my eyes—and listen to the same ugly bulletins over and over again from different radio stations. I can tell you it is a profound relief every night at midnight to talk to Alfred on the telephone and hear of the audience's response. It becomes more and more emphatic."

The news was black indeed and darkened day by day as the Nazi blitzkrieg swept across Europe, and a beleaguered England found herself alone. Sherwood listened to his radio with deepening despair. In spite of his bouts with melancholy, he was an optimist at heart. Now, even his optimism came near to deserting him. "I am at a mighty low ebb & so are the hopes of the human race. We may be on the verge of the unspeakable, unthinkable,

unbearable.'' Sherwood was a tired man still living in
two worlds, pleased of course by the success of his play
but drawn more and more away from the theatre by his
ever-swelling absorption in the tragic turn of world affairs.

Maxwell Anderson, a fellow founder of the Playwrights' Company, understood Sherwood's dilemma. He
wrote, ''Sam Behrman tells me that a small flood of
vituperation reaches your mail-box because of your stand
in *There Shall Be No Night*—and that it worries you more
than it should, coming at a time when you're not only
ill but a good deal worn down by the burst of energy in
which you wrote the play and put it on. I just want to
say that I'm proud of you for having written it—for
having raised your voice and spoken out like a man at a
time when everybody else (including myself) was still
clinging to dubious hopes. It's seldom that anybody is so
prophetically accurate and right. Whether France wins
or loses there will soon be only crack-pots in disagreement.''

If Sherwood was ever downed by the sniping letters
his play provoked, it was not for long, and only in his
lowest moments of fatigue. He was a stubborn man. He
knew his mind. He had proudly stated his interventionist
point of view. Any outrage which *There Shall Be No
Night* may have caused isolationists was proof that he
had succeeded in saying effectively what he set out to say.
His mail was heavy. There were favorable—and protest-
ing—notices and news stories from around the country,
and praising notes from old theatrical friends. Among
these was Noel Coward who, having sat through the first

night in tears, said at its conclusion that his trip to America would have been worth while if he had had no other reason for making it.

More significant of his future were the letters Sherwood received from Washington. They were indications of the new esteem in which he was held by a new public. They came from the President, Mrs. Roosevelt, Harry Hopkins, and, among others highly placed, three Justices of the Supreme Court: Stone, who could not recall "a play of such power and beauty"; Murphy, who congratulated him "on a magnificent dramatic composition"; and Frankfurter, who wrote, "It is the artist's function to make his perceptions contagious, and that is what you have done superbly in your play."

In spite of such recognition and the sweet knowledge that he had a hit which was having many lively "repercussions," Sherwood remained despondent well into May. Then, when he was at his most despairing, William Allen White once again entered his life, this time in a way that was to alter his career. Back in October, Sherwood had served with White on the Non-Partisan Committee for Peace, which was disbanded in November after having done its effective bit in getting the Neutrality Law revised. Now White asked Sherwood to join the Committee to Defend America by Aiding the Allies, of which he was chairman and Clark M. Eichelberger, a dedicated worker for peace, the national director. Sherwood accepted at once and found his strength and spirits restored by his new activities. He was, as he had confessed to White in December, a convinced interventionist. White was for anything short of war. Both men, however, were as one in their conviction that a Nazi victory would spell disaster for this hemisphere and that the surest guarantee of the future safety of the United States lay in making all possible aid available to the imperiled Allies.

In his answer to White, Sherwood pointed out that Hitler might win "this war this year" and reduce Britain and France to the status of Poland and Scandinavia. "There is only one course open to us at this tragic moment," he maintained. "We must go to the Allies' aid with all the power that we can command. We can not send an army now . . . We can not send our navy . . . We can contribute money and materials, planes and guns and food, and we can pray to God that the British and French won't weaken in their will to fight for freedom."

Sherwood's letter to White was released on May 22. A month later, "Aiding the Allies" meant "Aiding Britain," because she was the only one of them that continued to govern in her own country. Among the many convinced that Britain was also bound to fall, and this within a matter of weeks, were General Weygand, Pierre Laval, and Marshal Pétain; Roosevelt's two top ambassadors, William C. Bullitt in Paris and Joseph P. Kennedy in London, and, most prominent and articulate in this country, Charles A. Lindbergh. These men underestimated Churchill, who on May 10 had replaced Chamberlain as Prime Minister. They underestimated the British people. They also underestimated Franklin D. Roosevelt.

An election year did not make the President's position easier. An election year in which he had to decide whether to break with tradition and run for a third term was an even greater challenge. Since Munich, Roosevelt had seen clearly that Hitler's triumphs were a menace to the United

States. Slowly he had been driven to the realization that the Allies were defending us by defending themselves. When France collapsed, he was the more determined to support Britain by finding ways of supplying her with arms and working out what eventually became the destroyers-for-bases deal. During this period, when many were sincerely isolationist, the President was compelled to advance cautiously. His problem was to prepare America to accept the moves which he knew he had to make. In persuading the public that all steps short of war should be taken, William Allen White played a vital part, aided by his Committee, which Sherwood had joined.

The Committee to Defend America by Aiding the Allies began as an improvisation by White and Clark Eichelberger which, under their direction, swiftly became a national organization. It was born of urgency and grew rapidly during May and June as one staggering European crisis followed another. By fall it had jumped to more than seven hundred local chapters with hundreds of thousands of members, including both Republicans and Democrats. Although Sherwood attended many meetings in New York during the first two months, his most notable contribution was made in the first two weeks. It was then that he wrote on his own the full-page, 1,000-word advertisement that was published in newspapers across the country on Monday, June 10, under the heading STOP HITLER NOW!

The actual preparation of the copy had begun six days before. At a meeting of the Playwrights' Company on Tuesday afternoon an excited Sherwood read an ad he wanted to rush through for the Defend America Committee. After dinner that night he and S. N. Behrman began working over the text and continued until 3:00 A.M. When Behrman asked how much it would cost, Sherwood drawled, "I haven't the faintest idea." He did not, but by Friday the amount was estimated at $24,000, of which Sherwood paid a substantial part.

Once started, things moved rapidly. On June 5 Sherwood took the copy to a printer. On the 6th he submitted the proof to Eichelberger and some other Committee members, who decided to print the ad in the Committee's name, with William Allen White as national chairman. On the 7th it was scheduled for publication through an advertising agency. On the 10th it appeared in papers up and down the country and, when displayed in the windows of the national headquarters on West Fortieth Street, drew crowds of volunteers. On that day the New York Chapter delivered at the White House petitions bearing 25,000 signatures. On the next, the day after Mussolini declared war on France and Roosevelt delivered his "stab in the back" speech at Charlottesville, the President held his semiweekly press conference in Washington. There, in the presence of two hundred correspondents, with the tear sheets on his desk, he made an extraordinary reference to the advertisement.

Questioner: "Do you care to comment on the page ad today, put out by the Committee—"

The President (interposing): "Bill White's?"

Questioner: "Yes, sir."

The President: "Well, I had not read it and I read this morning that Bob Sherwood wrote it so I read it then. It is a great piece of work, extremely educational for the people of this country and, without going into a specific endorsement of every phase, it is a mighty good thing that Bill White and his Committee are getting things like that out for the education of this country."

Sherwood addressed a vast number of Americans when he wrote his advertisement, and in the process spoke for himself in a new way. The propagandist replaced the dramatist, the recruiting officer the writer of dialogue. Long as his copy was, his manner was jabbingly direct, as in the excerpts which follow.

STOP HITLER NOW!

We Americans have naturally wished to keep out of this war—to take no steps which might lead us in. But—

We now know that every step the French and British fall back brings war and world revolution closer to US—our country, our institutions, our homes, our hopes for peace. . . .

If Hitler wins in Europe—if the strength of the British and French armies and navies is forever broken—the United States will find itself alone in a barbaric world—a world ruled by Nazis, with "spheres of influence" assigned to their totalitarian allies. . . .

We have ample cause for deepest alarm. It should impel us, not to hysteria, but to resolute action. . . .

The Monroe Doctrine is not an automatic safety catch, securing the entrance to our hemisphere from all intruders. We have to enforce it—all the way from Greenland and Alaska to Cape Horn. Furthermore, we have to guard night and day against the manifold enemies from within. We can not ignore the fact that Trojan horses are grazing in all the fertile fields of North and South America. . . .

We can and should and will devote ourselves to a vast program of defense. . . .

This is a job for *all* of us! It will take years for us to build the necessary machines and to train the men who will run them. Will the Nazis considerately wait until we are ready to fight them?

Anyone who argues that they will wait is either an imbecile or a traitor. . . .

Whatever our feelings about the tragic mistakes of statesmanship in England and France we know now that the free people of those nations are willing to fight with inspiring heroism to defend their freedom. We know now that such men will die rather than surrender. . . .

There is nothing shameful in our desire to stay out of war, to save our youth from the dive bombers and the flame throwing tanks in the unutterable hell of modern warfare.

But is there not an evidence of suicidal insanity in our failure to help those who now stand between us and the creators of this hell?

WE CAN HELP—IF WE WILL ACT NOW

—before it is forever too late.

We can help by sending planes, guns, munitions, food. We can help to end the fear that American boys will fight and die in another Flanders, closer to home.

The members of our government are your servants. In an emergency as serious as this, they require the expression of your will. They must know that the American people are not afraid to cast off the hypocritical mask of neutrality, which deceives no one, including ourselves.

Send a postcard, a letter, or a telegram, at once—to the President of the United States, to your Senators and your Congressmen—urging that the *real* defense of our country must begin NOW—with aid to the Allies!

The United States of America is still the most powerful nation on earth—and the United States of America is YOU!

The advertisement, having been written for the Committee, stated its point of view and White's. Only once in it did Sherwood make it clear that he was prepared to go further. This was when, with an intemperance which horrified the elderly Kansan, he said that anyone who argued that the Nazis would wait until we were ready to fight was "either an imbecile or a traitor." Four days after the ad appeared, White wrote Sherwood in alarm about the offending words. "You are bringing my gray hairs in sorrow to the grave. Since the advertisement came out the ratio of critical letters has been multiplied so heavily that I have been unable to get through my day's work with three stenographers. . . . Of course there are millions of Americans who honestly believe in the isolationist theory. I don't; you don't. But when you call them imbeciles or traitors they rush to the nearest desk and write me letters which often are so intelligent that they have to be answered. And worse than that, they write to Roosevelt—which is Bad Medicine. This letter is written in the hope that if the advertisement goes out again that paragraph can be lifted and milder, more tolerant language used."

Sherwood was at Dartmouth receiving an honorary degree when White's letter reached New York. Immediately on his return he wrote that he was "shocked" to hear of the response White had had and promised that, if the ad were run again, the unfortunate phrase would be changed. "It does no good to say, 'I didn't mean to—.' The fact that you have heard so much from it proves that the meaning wasn't clear, and that is a serious mistake in an advertisement or other form of literary composition." He admitted that the launching of the ad was "perhaps an action of undue temerity" on his part, but the time was short, the New York Committee approving, and action needed.

Though Sherwood had gone further in the one phrase

than White was willing to, he would have gone much further throughout had he been stating his own point of view. He made this clear the day the ad appeared when his part in it became known and the newspapers sought him out. "Tall, grave, earnest," according to a New York *Herald Tribune* reporter, "he appeared more like a thoughtful young professor than a Broadway playwright noted for satiric comedy. He spoke slowly with his well-known measured cadence which gave sincerity and emphasis to his words." Speaking for himself, he said he believed it would be common sense to declare war at once on the side of Britain and France regardless of our unpreparedness. His reason was that "the moral effect would be absolutely overwhelming. It would be the greatest contribution we could make. No material aid we could give would ever count as heavily." He recalled his own experiences in the First War when he was serving in France with the Canadian Black Watch. Months after our entry into the war, there was no American army; there were no planes, no guns in France, but "there was the overwhelming faith that we were on the way." He also stated his belief—saying this was a very important thing to him—that this time we must go in "with our eyes open to the consequences" and, after Hitler's defeat, "assume our responsibility in keeping the peace."

Except for the offending words, White saluted the advertisement as "a masterpiece" that he would like to see run in every paper in the country. As a matter of fact, it was published in over one hundred cities. The excitement it created and the comment it won, however, did not lessen the difference between Sherwood's and White's stand. Each man liked and admired the other;

both men strongly favored aiding the Allies. But where the editor from Emporia would not budge beyond assistance short of war, the playwright-turned-public-spokesman advocated our becoming a belligerent without delay. Although they walked down the same path, the older man could not bring himself to go the whole way.

Increasingly in the months ahead, White wanted to make his position unmistakable. The more explicit he became in speaking for himself, the more irked the younger members of his Committee became by having him speak for them. By December, 1940, their discontent had blown into near-mutiny, and among those unhappy was Sherwood, though by then he had long since stopped his more active work with the Committee.

The flare-up came when White learned that Roy Howard planned to strafe him and his organization in the Scripps-Howard newspapers. White was old and tired, worried about his wife's health, and worn down by being identified as a warmonger. Part of his great reputation was based on his being ahead, but not too far ahead, of public opinion. He wanted to safeguard that reputation. Accordingly, he wrote Howard a long, placating letter in which he said, "If I was making a motto for the Committee to Defend America by Aiding the Allies, it would be 'The Yanks Are Not Coming.'"

When published by Howard with White's permission, this letter created a furor. It delighted White's opponents and distressed his friends. It closed the door on actions which the future might require and made the unconsulted committee a party to White's commitment. Among the overjoyed were General Robert E. Wood, chairman of the America First Committee, and Charles A. Lindbergh.

Among the aghast were such members of White's executive committee as Lewis W. Douglas, Herbert Bayard Swope, Ulric Bell, Thomas K. Finletter, and Eichelberger. Their protests were so strong and White's reaction to them so unyielding that early in January the old gentleman resigned. Sherwood was no less upset. He also felt that White, "harassed and harried" by Howard, had gone too far in binding the Committee to his own non-interventionism.

Since his despairing letter to White, Sherwood had been convinced that we should enter the war. Other members of the Defend America Committee felt no less free to go beyond White. Six of them, in fact, were among the thirty signers of a petition asking for an immediate declaration of war, which appeared on the same day as the ad. Although not among the signers, Sherwood was with them in spirit. He had become an involved man, free because of the success of *There Shall Be No Night* to devote himself to working with those who were alerting America to the dangers of Hitler.

The White Committee was not enough for him. In the crucial spring and summer months of 1940 he met for bi-weekly dinners with a group of men dedicated to organizing active aid for Britain, beginning with the destroyers-for-bases deal. Often known as "the Miller Group" because of the work done for it by Francis P. Miller of the Council on Foreign Relations, and also identified as "the Century Group" since its dinners were held in a private room on the top floor of the Century Association, it was the nucleus of the Fight for Freedom Committee, which was to emerge the next year. Although it cooperated with the White Committee, it was eyed with

THE ORDEAL OF A PLAYWRIGHT

suspicion by the old gentleman. Its members were too
young in their thinking to bring comfort to his age. To
him they were going too far too fast. To Sherwood they
were headed at the right pace for the right goal and were
a part of his introduction to a new world.

The great debate was noisy in the land, the debate
which would be silenced only by the bombs the Japanese
dropped on Pearl Harbor. It was a battle fought with
words, often angry and bitter words, for the mind of an
America sharply divided between those who believed that
the war against Hitler was our war and those who believed that it was not. Sherwood, very much convinced
that it was our war, threw himself at once and unremittingly into convincing others.

By late September, 1940, he wrote his mother, "I am
on ten or more different committees. I have to write all
sorts of articles and speeches (for myself and other people). And my correspondence is so enormous that it's
enough of a chore just to look at it." At that time he had
scheduled for the next two weeks speeches at the World's
Fair, Hartford, the *Herald Tribune* Forum, and Engle-
wood, New Jersey, the last, it should be noted, at the
invitation of an approving Mrs. Dwight Morrow, Lindbergh's mother-in-law. In these new activities, important
among which was the Council for Democracy, a group
seeking to strengthen American institutions and oppose
subversive organizations, he took boyish pleasure in discovering that he could "exert influence." This he pro-
ceeded to do to the limit of his powers. On the radio, at
mass rallies, at small meetings, in newspaper interviews,
and in articles for such magazines as *Reader's Digest,
Life,* and *Ladies' Home Journal,* he emerged, it amused

him to say, as a "notorious propagandist." There was no question that he had acquired a carrying name. Or that people became interested in what he had to say on subjects other than the theatre.

During that summer Sherwood for the most part functioned as the advocate of the views of the various committees on which he served. On three occasions, however, he spoke out for himself with passion. The first of these was his address to the graduating class of Milton Academy on June 14;* the second his plea "Union Now" in *Life,* and the third his broadcast to the Canadian people.

Twenty-six years had passed since, as a beanpole of a boy, he spoke at his own commencement. He now returned to Milton as a distinguished alumnus of forty-four who, because of *There Shall Be No Night* and the "Stop Hitler" ad, was most decidedly in the news. Although his mustache had whitened, his hair was still glossy black. Yet young as he looked, his face was old in its grimness and his body tense with foreboding.

The night before, when taking the midnight train to Boston, he had heard of the fall of Paris, and the news seemed to him "the blackest in all history." With his "mind full of this terrible knowledge" he tore up the speech he had written and sat up all night in his compartment writing a new one which he hoped would be worthy. Milton held a special place in his heart, and he was determined to pull no punches in describing to the young men he would face "the obscure and terrible future" that lay ahead of them. After an unsparing indictment of the

---

* See pages 4-9 of *Mirror to His Times* for a full account.

irresponsibility of his own generation in the years following the First War, he quoted the George Herbert line,
"Dare to be true," which is the Milton motto. He added,
"You cannot 'Dare to be true' in a world ruled by Hitler.
You cannot dare to be free, or even to be human. You
can only dare to die." He described his speech as being
among the "gloomiest" commencement addresses ever
delivered. Its sole indulgence in optimism was his faith
that the goodness which is in man would survive and his
hope that the students he addressed would "see a world
in which men have at last found a way to live in peace."

The depression that engulfed Sherwood the day that
Paris fell had left him by the beginning of October. Bad
as things were, they were not as bad as they had threat-
ened to be, or bad enough to prevent Sherwood from em-
bracing a new cause. This time when he spoke for himself,
it was in a leading article in *Life* in which he argued that
America's future lay in the union of the English-speaking
peoples. The plan, known as Union Now, was the idea of
Clarence K. Streit, a dreamer undaunted and a good man
better than the world. As the *New York Times* correspondent in Geneva, Streit had covered the League of
Nations and, having observed its failures, was determined
to evolve an international organization which would
avoid its defects. For some years, in print, on the air,
and at meetings, he had been so eloquent in advocating
a union of the democracies that Sherwood had become one
of its most dedicated disciples. He had appeared in public
as Streit's champion even before he wrote the piece for
Life. He slaved over the article and, when he finished it,
wrote his mother, "I think it is the most important thing
I've ever written. It urges immediate union of the U.S.

and the British Empire. That has been my dream for twenty-two years—the one achievement by the human race which, above all others, I have hoped I should live to see.''

Union Now was castlebuilding on sands that were not there, but Sherwood did not mind being chided as a Utopian. Living with a dream was an essential part of him, yet he was a realist, too. It was this Sherwood who on August 25, six weeks before the *Life* article appeared, addressed the men and women of Canada in a broadcast subsequently relayed to the British Empire.

His speech was one of a series called "Let's Face the Facts," delivered at the invitation of Canada's Director of Public Information. It was the most moving, the most personal, and the hardest slugging of any of his public utterances that summer, and, because Henry Ford and Charles A. Lindbergh were the isolationists singled out for attack, it received the widest newspaper attention.

It had taken Sherwood almost a year to bring himself to make this attack on Lindbergh. He did not jettison his heroes easily. More than to most, they were necessary to him. He had never forgotten his pride in the slim, shy young man who by spanning the Atlantic had conquered the world. With everyone's compassion he had followed the kidnapping, the Hauptmann trial, and the self-imposed exile into which the Lindberghs were forced as fugitives from their fame. He was aware that the Colonel had visited Hitler's Reich three times with seeming enjoyment and had accepted from Goering the second highest German decoration. He knew too that the Lindberghs, because of their admiration for the Luftwaffe, had been increasingly charged with being pro-Nazi. Even so, as late as January, 1939, Sherwood had not lost his enthusiasm for them. During a South American cruise with Madeline he read Anne Lindbergh's *Listen, the Wind* and noted, "She's a writer who deserves that grievously misused and overused adjective, 'divine.' It makes me sick to think of the way the Lindberghs have been excoriated as pro-Nazis—shows how unbalanced people have become on that awful subject."

Eight months later, Sherwood changed his mind, and it was Lindbergh himself who forced him to do so. On the night of September 15 he listened to the Colonel as he delivered the first of his radio addresses, and he was horrified. "It was profoundly shocking. Not only did he urge U.S. to keep out of war, but he said that if we went in we should lose a million men, maybe several million, and expend all our resources. If it takes that to beat Germany, then England and France are certainly doomed. He urged Americans to disbelieve all war news & propaganda (meaning British & French) whether it came from without the country or within. When we hear anything on the air or read it in a newspaper, of a partisan nature, we should enquire into the ownership of that paper or broadcasting chain. This sounds like outright anti-Semitism. The most awful part of this was that the speech, or parts of it, sounded lyrical, as though it had been written by Anne Lindbergh. . . . Feeling rather sick since hearing Lindbergh. That speech will be hailed ecstatically in Germany."

Only once in print, as far as I know, did Sherwood comment on this talk, and then most mildly in a letter to *Time*. *Time* had said that in his broadcast Lindbergh represented "everybody." Sherwood protested, "I beg to say he did not represent me.'' Most decidedly he did not. From the outset Sherwood's disagreement with him was fundamental; by the time of the Canadian address it had deepened into disgust. That was eleven months later, during which Lindbergh had delivered five major broadcasts, emerged as Roosevelt's chief competitor on the radio, and established himself as the country's leading spokesman for isolationism. In the process he had become anathema to Sherwood.

Although Sherwood had had the Colonel in mind in his ''Stop Hitler'' ad, he had been careful not to name him in his public statements. In his Canadian address he not only named him but damned him in the most unrestrained, Coughlinesque terms. The purpose of his speech was to hearten Canadians by assuring them that we were their fellows in a common cause and already at war. With deep feeling he recalled his experiences in the Canadian Black Watch in the First War and slashed out at the inhuman fallacies of Hitlerism. He insisted that the voice of the United States was expressed ''truly and eloquently'' by Roosevelt and Willkie, and not by ''Lindbergh or any other bootlicker of Adolph Hitler.'' There were important men in America, said Sherwood, who had ''succumbed to the demoralizing, degenerative influence of Hitlerism.'' In Sherwood's phrase, they were chiefly ''worshipers of the machine'' who, with their liking for Nazi regimentation, represented to him and many other Americans ''a traitorous point of view.''

As a former pacifist himself, Sherwood did not question the Colonel's right to be a pacifist or the sincerity of his beliefs. What appalled him was Lindbergh's seeming unawareness of the evil that was Hitlerism, his indifference to the freedoms of which Nazism was the murderer, his failure to take into account the spirit of the British people, and the eloquence with which he argued from false premises to false conclusions. In the course of following Lindbergh's broadcasts, with outrage which grew into disgust, Sherwood had lost a hero and found a villain.*

---

* It was not until eight years later, when the war was three years over, that Sherwood publicly softened his attitude toward the Colonel. Then in *Roosevelt and Hopkins*, page 155, he wrote, "As a footnote on Lindbergh, who had derided Roosevelt's call for 50,000 war planes as 'hysterical chatter': he eventually proved himself highly useful in experimental work for the Air Force; his precise recording mind retained all the intelligence material that had been so hospitably offered to him in Germany and he applied it effectively; he rendered valuable service as a civilian flyer testing some of the more than 300,000 war planes that this nation actually did produce before victory in 1945."

In fairness, it should be added that Lindbergh, who had resigned his commission in the Air Force early in 1941, offered his services after Pearl Harbor, saying, "Now that war has come, we must meet it as united Americans regardless of our attitude in the past." Upon being refused, he served with valor and distinction in the United States and in the Pacific as a technical consultant and test pilot for several aircraft companies (including Ford at Willow Run, ironically). In 1954, he was nominated by President Eisenhower and confirmed by the Senate as a Brigadier General in the Air Force Reserve.

· 5 ·

THE POWERHOUSE IS GONE

Early in August, 1940, Harry Hopkins was spending the
weekend with Mrs. Harvey Cushing at East Hampton,
Long Island, where the Sherwoods had rented a summer
house. Hopkins took Sherwood aside and asked, "What
are you warmongers up to now?"

Naturally, Sherwood, who describes the scene in *Roosevelt and Hopkins,* took it for granted that Hopkins was
joking. Even so, he gave a straight answer. He told Hopkins they were working on a campaign to transfer fifty
American overage destroyers to the British Navy. Hopkins assumed a look of disgust. "You mean you're going
to come right out publicly and ask the President to give
fifty of our fighting ships to a belligerent?"

Sherwood pointed out that these destroyers were of no
immediate use to us. They were lying idle and had been
for years. "But don't you realize," Hopkins asked, "that
a public demand like that would be a big embarrassment

to the President—especially now, with an election coming up?''

Sherwood replied that some of his associates were working privately to get Wendell Willkie's agreement to the proposal, which was in line with Roosevelt's whole policy. ''What do *you* know about the President's policy?'' demanded Hopkins. ''Don't you know that this country is neutral?'' Sherwood's anger was mounting by the minute, and he became more and more depressed at the thought that this man, so close to Roosevelt, was a narrow-minded isolationist.

''The whole country's isolationist,'' snarled Hopkins, ''except for a few pro-British fanatics like you. How do you imagine that the President could possibly justify himself with the people if he gave up fifty of our destroyers?'' Sherwood's answer was a tirade of greater vehemence than he could usually muster, his eloquence fueled by his rage. He insisted ''that the people were a lot less neutral than Hopkins seemed to think—that they hated Nazism—that if Roosevelt would speak to them with his own great courage and clarity they would support him, etc., etc.''

When he concluded, Hopkins grinned and said, ''All right then—why do you waste your breath shouting all this at *me*? Why don't you get out and say these things to the people?'' Sherwood realized at last that he had been completely taken in and that this was just Hopkins' special and devious way of finding out if he had ''any real arguments to support his emotional bias.''

Sherwood had first met Hopkins two years earlier. He was interested in him, entertained by him, and recognized his shrewdness. But something about him put Sherwood off. Perhaps it was the braggart's quality of some of his phrases. Since then, he had seen a lot of Hopkins and their acquaintance had deepened into friendship. Having met him only socially, however, he had not yet learned that Hopkins, an inveterate tease, enjoyed goading those with whom he worked.

Two months later he again encountered his frail friend's working methods. Early in October when Hopkins was staying at Essex House in New York, he asked Sherwood to come by and see him for reasons that he did not explain. When he arrived, Hopkins told him the President had to give a speech on Columbus Day. "It's supposed to be one of those routine State Department speeches about Western Hemisphere solidarity, directed primarily to South America. But the President wants to talk to the American people about Hitler. So far as he is concerned, there is absolutely nothing important in the world today but to beat Hitler."

According to Sherwood, Hopkins looked at him sharply as though expecting him to dispute this point. It was another trap but one into which he did not fall. When he did not, Hopkins asked him, "What do you think the President ought to say?" Sherwood was understandably flabbergasted. He aired a few views, which were discussed back and forth. Then Hopkins said, "Come on, let's go and see Sam Rosenman," who lived only a few blocks away on Central Park West.

When he found himself at the Rosenmans' apartment for lunch, Sherwood was still in the dark, though he assumed that the Columbus Day speech was to be discussed. He had met the Judge at a party after the opening of *Abe Lincoln,* but to him he was "one of those vague fig-

ures in the background of the Roosevelt palace guard.''
He did not know of Rosenman's closeness to the President or that he had served him as a speech writer since the days in Albany. He made this clear while he and the Rosenmans were talking after lunch, waiting for Hopkins to return from his mandatory nap.

He said that he had been reading a great many of Roosevelt's speeches as Governor and President and was struck by the continuity and uniformity of their style. He added that he was sure the President must have written all of these himself because, if there had been any substantial assistance, they would have a mixed quality which would show up right away. The Judge reports in *Working with Roosevelt* that he and Mrs. Rosenman were amused by this naïveté but said nothing, pleased as they were to have the hard work done by many on the President's speeches fool a professional writer of Sherwood's standing.

Within the hour, when Hopkins rejoined them after his rest, Sherwood learned the hard facts of presidential speech writing. The three men started discussing the notes Roosevelt had dictated, the State Department draft, and the new ideas that ought to be added. Sherwood became so interested that he forgot to be awed and even started arguing. Rosenman was impressed by the clarity with which he expressed his ideas; he was convinced that the playwright was sympathetic to the President's objectives. Abruptly, the Judge slapped a pencil on the table and said, ''Well, gentlemen—there comes a time in the life of every speech when it's got to be written. . . . Suppose, Mr. Sherwood, you go into the dining room and write a couple of paragraphs about isolationists in America so that Harry and I can take a look at it. I'd like to write something about what Hitler is trying to do here in America along the 'divide and conquer' line.''

Sherwood looked at the Judge, ''mystified as if to say, 'What in the world is the use of my writing a couple of paragraphs up here in this apartment in New York City? How is that going to do any good in a speech that the President is now writing in Washington to be delivered in Dayton?' '' But, instead of saying what Rosenman was sure was in his mind, Sherwood pulled his six feet seven out of the chair, picked up a pack of cigarettes, and with a shrug of his shoulders went to work.

When the first day's drafting was done, Hopkins returned to Washington. Sherwood and Rosenman worked on the speech for the next few evenings, doing their writing in separate rooms and then meeting to criticize each other's material. As their discussions continued, what had been a routine Columbus Day statement was converted into a speech in defense of the President's foreign policy. On October 9 the Judge with their latest draft in hand headed for the White House to go over the speech with the President, returned to New York the next day, and invited Sherwood to come to his apartment to listen to the final version on the radio on Saturday night. Sherwood's eager question was, ''What did the President think of our draft?'' Rosenman's answer was that, though there were some parts he wanted to change, he liked most of it. From long experience the Judge added that the best way to determine what the President thought was to listen and see how much he used. ''I'll be there,'' said Sherwood.

He sat before the radio with a carbon of their version in his hands, still convinced that their work would prove in vain. Then suddenly Roosevelt was on the air. His familiar voice, patrician but neighborly, and comforting in its confidence, filled the room. It was the same Roosevelt he had heard a hundred times, but this time there was an all-important difference. Many of the words the President was speaking were Sherwood's. As Sherwood followed the copy in front of him, his lips moved unconsciously and his face lit up with delight. He was experiencing the thrill of hearing his words spoken by the President of the United States. His pleasure was so visible that Rosenman shared in it. The Judge well knew that the thrill of the first time was always the deepest for presidential speech writers. As a playwright, Sherwood had spent his life listening to famous actors speak his lines. But, as he said to Rosenman, "when Roosevelt does it—it's different."

Sherwood linked his going to work at the White House directly to his conversation with Hopkins at Mrs. Cushing's. The connection, though direct, included an element of chance that was unknown to him. By October Thomas Corcoran and Benjamin Cohen, who for years had worked with Rosenman, were no longer helping with the President's speeches. The 1940 campaign was at hand, and Hopkins and Rosenman were urgently in need of another writer. The first name they thought of was Raymond Gram Swing, the famous radio commentator. On learning he was out of the country, Hopkins suggested his new friend Sherwood, who had won the President's attention by his "Stop Hitler" ad and his *Abe Lincoln* film. The Judge, familiar with Sherwood's plays and his work for the White Committee, acquiesced, and they determined to try him out on the Dayton speech.

Sherwood's passing this test was a turning point in his career. It marked his induction into working for Roosevelt and the beginning of the writing team of Hopkins, Rosenman, and Sherwood. During the next four and a half years until the President's death, there were others, notably Archibald MacLeish, who assisted from time to time. It was, however, Hopkins, Rosenman, and Sherwood who worked most closely with Roosevelt on all of his major speeches. On a few occasions one or another was ill or out of the country, but one of the trio was always present.

Those four and a half years found Sherwood at the center of most of the most dramatic situations in history. No doubt he had occasion to reflect that everything that had happened to him since 1940 was in the nature of a sequel to *There Shall Be No Night,* with Sherwood himself on stage as one of the principal actors. And the most dramatic scene of all was the passing of F.D.R.

We rarely know when a time will be the last one. Certainly Sherwood neither knew nor suspected, when he wrote Harry Hopkins early in April, 1945, about having recently had "one very pleasant lunch" with the President, that the lunch on March 23 would be the final one. He had looked forward to lunching with the President that Friday. He had not seen him since his fourth Inauguration nine weeks earlier and the small dinner at the White House the next night, at which F.D.R. had chosen to celebrate his sixty-third birthday in advance because of his imminent departure for Yalta.

Undoubtedly, it had been pleasant to be with the President again on those terms of intimacy which both men had relished in the past. Yet there was something about this meeting which saddened Sherwood when it was over, something which he left undefined, a sense of change for which he was not prepared.

He had realized the White House would be different, with Pa Watson dead and Hopkins ill at the Mayo Clinic. Sherwood's affection for Watson, after whom he thought of naming the destroyer in his play *The Rugged Path,* was genuine. So was the President's. The death on the *Quincy* of this big, florid, jovial, yet devastatingly astute Virginian on the way home from Yalta had been an awful blow for Roosevelt. According to Sherwood, F.D.R. was not in the habit of sharing his personal sorrows. He had not let anyone know his feelings when his mother died and had been unwilling to talk about her death. He was equally silent and undemonstrative after the deaths of his old friends and associates, Louis Howe, Marvin McIntyre, and Missy LeHand. But he did not even try to hide his grief when he lost Pa Watson. In Sherwood's words, "the very extent to which he talked about his sadness gave alarm to those who knew him best, because it suggested that he himself was failing."

Harry Hopkins' having left the *Quincy* on the same homeward voyage at Algiers because of illness had inconvenienced, disappointed, and displeased F.D.R. He suspected Hopkins of simply fearing boredom. He was certain that he would get better medical care on the cruiser than at Marrakech, where he went for a four-day rest before flying to Washington and then on to the Mayo Clinic. Furthermore, he could not believe, as an Eternal Naval Person, that anyone could feel bad on a ship. The result was that Roosevelt's leavetaking with his valued and devoted friend was not exactly cordial. This was worse than unfortunate, since they were not to meet again.

Sherwood was luckier at his last meeting with the President. The day was good; the war news even better. The papers that morning carried heart-lifting headlines. The Nazis, collapsing on both fronts, reeled in the west from a mammoth air attack by the Americans and a big push by Montgomery, and in the east from a crushing drive by the Russians in Silesia. The Tokyo radio reported a United States fleet off the Ryukyus and nearing Okinawa. Two days before, Task Force 58 under the command of Sherwood's recent hosts, Admirals Spruance and Mitscher, had pushed its way into Japanese inland waters and, without losing a ship, had sunk fifteen warships and destroyed 475 planes. A week earlier, after almost a month of bitter and bloody fighting, a base for American planes had been gained on Iwo Jima, 750 miles from Yokohama. Victory was in the air. It was no longer a question of *if* the war would be won but a matter of *when*.

To be sure, he had heard reports about Yalta's having been a failure, about Stalin's having duped Churchill and Roosevelt, and about secret agreements made there that would imperil the peace and weaken the organization of the United Nations. In Washington, where gossip blows on the calmest days, he had also heard disturbing rumors about the President's health. He had seen pictures of him taken at Yalta and on the *Quincy*. He knew that F.D.R. had delivered his Yalta speech to Congress sitting down, explaining at the outset (in what Sherwood thought incorrectly to be the only public reference he ever made to his infirmity) that it was a lot easier for him to be seated than to carry about ten pounds of steel around on the bottom of his legs. Naturally, this had added to the rumors, all of which Sherwood discounted.

Sherwood needed to believe that the world would regain sanity and peace after the madness and anguish of war. It was not because he was a dramatist that he felt a happy ending must be at hand. It was because he was a decent, rational, civilized man who, along with millions of his kind the globe over, was convinced that the results of victory would justify the sacrifices of the war. As he was to write his Aunt Jane in England early the next month, "this time it certainly seems that we have learned —at awful cost but with awful clarity—all that we failed to learn after 1918." He took it for granted that Roosevelt would live to give order to the victory he had done so much to make possible.

Sherwood knew that with his withdrawal from official life he would be more out of touch with the President after their luncheon than he had ever been during their previous separations. He was ready to continue helping with the speech writing on such occasions as his services might be needed. Yet, denied the intimacies of daily association, shared work, and sustaining trivia, he recognized that the relationship he enjoyed with the President was bound to change, though their friendship remained secure.

Forrestal had this widely known friendship in mind when he said to a lieutenant after Sherwood's safe return from the Pacific,* "If anything had happened to Bob, instead of getting a promotion you would have ended up

---

* Editor's Note: Early in 1945, Sherwood was sent to Guam by F.D.R. to assess the degree to which United States military officials in the Pacific area were able to anticipate the flow of events.

in Portsmouth prison.'' It was as ''my old friend'' that the President had described Sherwood in his letter of introduction to General Douglas MacArthur. As such a friend, Sherwood approached the White House. His mood was buoyant. Though still tired from his Pacific trip, he remained so exhilarated by what he had seen that his exhilaration routed his fatigue. This time he had a new bond with the President. He, a Black Watch infantryman from 'way back, could now talk with Roosevelt as a Navy enthusiast.

Sherwood met the President in his office and walked beside him as he was wheeled over to the White House proper. There they took the elevator to the third floor and were joined for luncheon by F.D.R.'s daughter Anna on the sun porch above the South Portico. The sun porch, once a playroom, had in the Roosevelts' later years been reclaimed for the President's use. Next to it a kitchen had been installed which was presided over by Mary Campbell, an Irish cook who had been with Mrs. James Roosevelt until her death. F.D.R. liked this glassed-in Shangri-la because of its cheerful intimacy. Mary Campbell was another reason that he liked it. She was an old-fashioned cook who could really cook, who believed in thick cream and tempting sauces, whose cooking the President relished, especially since he had no fondness for the food served downstairs.

The President was delighted to have news of his two sons in the Pacific, Sherwood having seen James in the Philippines and been told by his skipper that John was doing a good job on his airplane carrier. He was also delighted with the ''Tell-him-that-I-love-him'' message that Sherwood brought from Ernie Pyle and with the photograph (signed by Admirals Nimitz, Turner, and Spruance and General Smith) of the Marines raising the flag on Mount Suribachi. Nimitz had given this photograph to Sherwood on Guam and asked him to deliver it to the President along with a copy of the booklet *Morning Stars and Missionary Packet,* for which the Admiral had written a foreword.

Sherwood and the President talked of many things. Inevitably, the main topic was the war in the Pacific, and particularly General MacArthur, with whom Sherwood to his unhidden amazement was deeply impressed. He reported on the excellence of the General's intelligence service, the high quality and morale of his troops, and the magnificence of his military operations. He confessed, however, that he was shocked by the inaccurate views of both the General and his staff on the formation of policy in Washington, by the "unmistakable evidences of an acute persecution complex at work," and by "the most unfortunate public relations policy" he had seen in any theatre of war. He also spoke of the impression MacArthur had left with him that the Russians would be in the war in force against the Japanese before our own planned invasion of the home islands.

The President's special request had been for Sherwood to obtain the General's views on the occupation of Japan. Sherwood confessed that quite frankly he had been as surprised by the "remarkable liberalism" of these views as he had been impressed by MacArthur's eloquence in stating them. He said, therefore, that, though he had no idea who would be supreme commander when the forces under MacArthur and Nimitz were merged for the final assault, he believed strongly that MacArthur was the ideal choice for Military Governor of Japan after the surrender. When Sherwood added that MacArthur had told him victory over Japan was much nearer than Sherwood had realized, the President observed a trifle wistfully, "I wish he would sometimes tell some of these things to *me*." Roosevelt then asked Sherwood to prepare a short memorandum of his observations on MacArthur but told him to make no mention of the Russians, since that was a matter of the deepest security at that time.

They also talked about two speeches that the President was to deliver after his forthcoming visit to Warm Springs. The first was the Jefferson Day speech, which was due in about three weeks, and a rough draft of which the President handed him to work on. The second was the opening address at the San Francisco conference of the United Nations at which, F.D.R. confided laughingly, he planned to risk all by arriving at the start and staying to the end, in spite of Steve Early's advice that he appear only on the closing day and then only if the conference was a success. In regard to Jefferson, Roosevelt made the point that he was a scientist as well as a democrat and, without mentioning the atomic age that was almost at hand, asked Sherwood to look up some of Jefferson's statements on science. He did this later, incorporating them in the draft he sent to Warm Springs, and the one that pleased the President most referred to "the brotherly spirit of science, which unites into one family all its votaries of whatever grade, and however widely dispersed throughout the globe."

Sherwood had no way of knowing that the speech in

which this quotation was included would never be delivered. He did know that things at lunch were very different from what they had been. The President was in much worse shape physically than he had ever seen him before. His face was thinner and grayer, the circles under his eyes were menacingly dark, the old gaiety was subdued, the tremendous energy absent, the easy give-and-take lacking. Though the President had "perked up a little . . . under the sparkling influence of his daughter," he seemed "unnaturally quiet and even querulous," and Sherwood found himself in the strange position of carrying on most of the conversation. This had not happened before.

Though he sensed the President's extreme exhaustion, Sherwood was not alarmed by it. It never occurred to him that this time Roosevelt would not rally after a rest as he always had. His powers of recovery were extraordinary, his reserves of strength seemingly without limit. Sherwood took heart in the thought that the President was to have a vacation at Warm Springs and that thereafter he had ahead of him, in the journey to San Francisco, the kind of long train trip which had never failed to refresh him in the past. Accordingly, Sherwood wished the President a happy holiday with no premonition that these were the words of a final farewell rather than a temporary parting. As he left, Roosevelt was starting to read Nimitz's foreword.

Sherwood went down to the Cabinet Room, where he had worked for so many long hours with Hopkins and Rosenman, to write the brief memorandum the President had requested on MacArthur. He wrote it swiftly with his usual ease. Back at the Carlton he told Madeline in detail about his lunch, reporting candidly on the President's condition yet with no apprehension.

The Sherwoods left on the three o'clock train the next day. Sentimentally, Sherwood may have regretted bringing to an end those eventful years when he had worked at the White House close to history and to a maker of it he so hugely admired. Even so, he was happy to be out of the frictions of government service and anxious to pick up his own life and career.

Being back home with Madeline in their apartment at 25 Sutton Place, after the many dislocations and separations of the war years, was a joy in itself. The fact that Madeline, a happy and expert housekeeper, was doing all the cooking and housework, and finding it less tiring than coping with the servant problem, only added to the coziness of Sherwood's homecoming. Several times during these first three weeks his diary mentions dinners at home "cooked by darling," with the menus carefully noted and the food warmly praised. Among these dinners at home alone was the "lovely" one on April 4, Sherwood's forty-ninth birthday.

There were other welcome proofs of normal life reestablished. There was the pleasure of seeing Gaggy again and sharing with her his tales of the South Pacific, and of dining with such old friends as Ellin Berlin, Peggy Pulitzer, the Harold Guinzburgs, Adrianne Allen and Bill Whitney, and Marcia Davenport. There was the pleasure, too, of going once more with Madeline to such favorite restaurants as Chateaubriand, 21, the Plaza, or the Oak Room at the St. Regis. Of having Mary at home for Easter. And of lunching at the Century or the Golden Horn with such colleagues as Lou Cowan, Joe

Barnes, or Vic Samrock, all of whom later remembered Sherwood as being exhilarated in spite of being exhausted.

They remember his delight at being out of government work, his not wanting to talk politics, and his eagerness to discuss books, movies, and the theatre. They recalled the excitement with which he told his experiences in the Pacific and the pride with which he spoke of America's performance in the war. It was the same exuberant pride in our generals, our admirals, our servicemen, and in F.D.R. that led him to write Hopkins at this time, "It is difficult not to be an eagle-screaming, flag-waving chauvinist."

Sherwood had problems to face as well as pleasures to renew. The problems were psychological, financial, and professional. He had to unwind. He had to get "the war ants out of his pants." He had earned much in experience and little in money during his years in government service. He had been depleted financially and, as he wrote his Aunt Jane, had to "do a lot to try to restore some measure of solvency." He had to live up to a great reputation, which is harder than having to live a bad one down. He had wandered far afield of the theatre into larger zones of action and had to find his way back to his neglected acres. He had to get journalism out of his system and propaganda off his mind. Most difficult of all, he had to regain his touch as a playwright after five years during which he had written no plays.

"You Can't Go Back to Pocatello" was the title for an article Richard L. Neuberger once suggested to Jonathan Daniels, Pocatello being the home town in Idaho to which a defeated Senator found it impossible to return after tasting the richer fare of Washington. The question with Sherwood was: Could he go back to his Pocatello, which happened to be Broadway?

A first-rate secretary is one reason that some men come to be known as "indispensable." A secretary of one's own is not only a creator of order but a stern daily reminder of work to be done. On his return to New York, Sherwood was happy to find, as he had hoped he would, that Grace Murphy was already working for him as his secretary. This was the beginning of an association that lasted until her marriage nine years later.

Miss Murphy, a trim, bright, attractive young woman from Connecticut, had met Sherwood four years before in Washington at the Office of War Information and worked for him briefly before he went to London in 1944. Expert as she was, "scared to death" during the first week she took Sherwood's dictation, because she was afraid that the language he would use as a dramatist might be very different from what she was accustomed to. Sherwood himself had reason to wonder if he could find again this different language, knowing that he must.

He edged his way back into playwriting, with misgivings but without alarm. In those days Miss Murphy worked at the Playwrights' Company, and Sherwood would turn up at 630 Fifth Avenue about noon after a late, leisurely breakfast and a careful reading of the morning papers, bringing her to be typed whatever he had written in longhand at home. He would look through his mail, lunch out, and then return to dictate answers to the mass of letters on his desk. There were lots of things to interfere with his playwriting. There were letters to be written to the families of the Navy men he had met in the Pacific. There was a quick trip to Washington for the American National Theatre Academy and a speech for the Urban League. There was a review to write for the new newspaper *PM,* in New York, of Ira Wolfert's *American Guerilla in the Philippines,* a book he warmly admired. There were the articles to be done for *Collier's* that would justify his trip to the Pacific.

All these were commitments of conscience. Strong as they were, they did not keep him from starting a play. This was a major concern and also a commitment of conscience because of the obligation he felt to the Playwrights' Company after so long an absence and silence. Within three weeks after his return from the Pacific and two weeks after his luncheon with the President, Sherwood was working on a play. Though dissatisfied with his first attempts, he no more questioned that with time he would regain his knack than that the President, after a rest at Warm Springs, would regain his strength. His diary speaks for him.

April 6: At 6:32 P.M., I started writing. With time out for dinner I worked until about 2:00 A.M., knocking out 26 pages of Act I. I feel I have a pretty good start on the characters, but I don't know if this play is really going any place. It looks like a warming up, after more than five years of no practice, but at least it seems to have some vitality even if it proves to be crap. One thing in its favor -it's capable of all kinds of change and expansion, if that would help.

April 7: Stayed home all day to work, but wrote only 9 pages. Got out dear diary of 1940 and was amazed to read of the period of writing of *There Shall Be No Night.* I took nearly three weeks on the first draft of that, but the real work was done later, on the typing & on the rewriting after the Lunts had agreed to do it. It's appalling how much work I poured into that play, & I wonder if I'll be able to pour anything like the same amount into this one. I don't seem to feel tremendously interested now. In fact, I feel that this may be one of those things that, when finished, I shall put into the bureau drawer and forget, like *Milk & Honey* or *Afterglow*. But, even if it's in that regrettable category, it may still be useful in getting me back into the playwrighting groove. "Warming up" may be the right term.

April 12, Thurs.: Wrote review of Wolfert book. At about 5:55 P.M., I was returning to 25 Sutton Place when a blonde lady burst out of an apartment on the ground floor and asked, "Have you heard the news?" She seemed so bewildered and bemused that I asked her, "What news?"—thinking that the 9th Army had entered Berlin, or something like that, and she said, "The President is dead." I asked her, "What President? The President of what?" I walked close to her, as though I were grilling her, like a District Attorney. She said, "President Roosevelt—it—it just came on the radio." She was so sort of wild, and indefinite—and she didn't seem the type to care, particularly—that I thought she must be crazy. I went up in the elevator, found a note from M. saying she was resting, & went to the radio. The terrible, unbelievable thing was true. I heard Fiorello. He was very fine. I couldn't bear to call my darling. The shock was awful, but merciful.

April 13, Fri.: This morning when I woke up the shock was repeated. (Last night we went to dine with Mario Harriman, & Paul Hollister called & asked me to write something & I was up most of the night writing it.) I went over what I had written, & typed, at breakfast. Then Paul came, about 9:15, & I gave it to him. Then I read the papers. The shock had passed, & its protection removed, and I felt defenseless, & I started to cry. I tried hard to control myself, but I couldn't stop the tears. All I could think of was that that lovely, kind, good, great person had been struck down at the moment when he and we were so close to the goals he had fought for, so gallantly and with such great vision, against such terrible opposition, at home & abroad. Harry Hopkins called, from Rochester, Minn. I listened to the CBS broadcast of what I had written. It was splendidly done by Tom Chalmers. At 4:30 we left for Washington.

Poor darling—on the train.

Wrote today to Mrs. R. & Pres. Truman. Also to Henry Morgenthau.

April 14, Sat.: At the Carlton, Lafayette Park—thunder. White House at 3:30 P.M. On the train for the final trip at 10:00 P.M.

Talk with Harry at his house at 6:00 P.M.

80 years ago Lincoln was shot.

April 15, Sun.: Arrived Hyde Park at 8:40. Burial service.

Lilacs—Walt Whitman.

Arrived Penn Station about 5:00.

Dinner at Mother's—but without darling, who felt awful.

It was inexpressibly sad, being on the train with Sam, Steve, Henry Wallace, Felix, Frank Walker and all the others—but not the President, for whom & in whom we have lived together. I looked around at the faces, there in the rose garden at Hyde Park, & thought what a vast range of Americans they covered—Gen. Marshall & Harry Hooker & Elmer van Waggener & Lubin & Mackenzie King & Vincent Astor & Dorothy Brady & Uncle Fred Delano—& I thought that there is nobody who ever knew him well who doesn't love him.* And I looked at that valiant figure, Eleanor Roosevelt, & Dorothy Brady & Uncle Fred Delano—& I thought that "class will tell." Champions come through in the pinches.

April 16, Mon.: Persuaded my darling to remain in bed while I fixed orange juice & coffee. Then washed dishes & did some scrubbing in kitchen and pantry with Babo.

Went to office & wrote some letters. Read F. Sullivan in *PM*, & cried again.

Listened at 1:00 P.M. to Truman's first speech as President. Thought it admirable, but a trifle too long.

My sweet, darling wife told me to write here that I have

---

* On second thought—there are undoubtedly some exceptions, like Raymond Moley. But they, thank God, are the exceptions which prove the rule.

been a wonderful husband today. I asked her to sign that: *Approved*. MADELINE.

It was characteristic of Sherwood to notice the lilacs, to think instantly of Lincoln and Whitman, and to record without embarrassment the tears that finally came. It was characteristic of him to see the democratic strength of Roosevelt, the man and the leader, in the diversity of those who mourned him in the Rose Garden, and to speak of "class" in connection with Mrs. Roosevelt in no snobbish sense but only in terms of her character, proud of her valor and of her for proving that "champions come through in the pinches."

No less characteristic of him was that, deep as was his grief, he was not fooled by the fakers among the many who flooded the airwaves with tributes. "It was a great comfort to me to hear your words," he wrote Mayor LaGuardia, "for you really knew what you were talking about. Later, on the radio, I heard numerous empty eulogies from phonies who had consistently opposed and obstructed Franklin D. Roosevelt in every progressive measure that he had championed, and it made me sick. But you were his real friend and the mighty exponent of his principles."

When Sherwood heard the "terrible, unbelievable" news of the President's death, he refused at first to accept as true what he had long dismissed as beyond possibility. So strong was his disbelief that three years later, when describing the moment in *Roosevelt and Hopkins*, he wrote, "Like everybody else, I listened and listened to the radio, waiting for the announcement—probably in his own gaily reassuring voice—that it had all been a big mistake, that the banking crisis and the war were over and everything was going to be 'fine—grand—perfectly bully.' But when the realization finally did get through all I could think was, 'It finally crushed him. He couldn't stand up under it any longer.' "

Sherwood had not had to call Madeline. She woke up within an hour after he came home and remembers what they felt rather than what they said. Marie Harriman, stunned by the news and alone because Averell was in Moscow as Ambassador, called and asked the Sherwoods for dinner at her Sixty-eighth Street apartment. She, like Madeline, recalls that the three of them ate little, talked little, and cried a lot as they listened to the radio and answered the endless telephone calls that came through, including the request from Paul Hollister that Sherwood write something about the President for CBS.

His tribute was read first on the radio at 11:40 on Friday morning by Thomas Chalmers and again that night at 10:07 by Raymond Massey. Playgoers heard it that same evening when the star of every play on Broadway read it after the final curtain. It was frankly a eulogy written, in the mood and language of wartime, from and for the needs and emotions of the moment. It was a vent for the agony of a man who talked best with his pen, the first outpouring of the great sorrow within him.

Hollister had asked him to write personally about the President, and Sherwood did. From his own experience he contrasted the jitters that shook Washington in the black hours and days after Pearl Harbor with the courage, serenity, and confidence of Roosevelt which he encountered whenever he went into the White House and "into the presence of the President himself." He recalled how the President would lean back in his chair, in his Oval Study on the second floor, and state very clearly and simply what he thought our military strategy should be, emphatically rejecting any defensive or defeatist policy, and insisting that we must go out and find the enemy, "and hit them—and hit them again."

He spoke of Roosevelt's love of the ships that were sunk or incapacitated at Pearl Harbor. "He knew them," Sherwood said, "and loved them. He had the Navy feeling about those ships—and he did not think of them merely as things built of steel—he always thought of ships as flesh and blood." Sherwood after his trip to the Pacific was able to add, "And that, of course, is what they are."

"I hesitate," he continued, "to speak now of my personal feelings at his death. I had the honor to be numbered among his friends—but that was a very large company. . . . He was a good man. He was a decent man. He was a friendly, patient, supremely tolerant man. . . . I have seen him goaded and insulted and driven beyond what seemed to be the limits of human endurance, but I have never seen him to be anything less than great under pressure. . . . I confess that I feel very sad at the thought that he will not live to realize his dearest dream, the fruition of his tremendous plans . . . for a practicable, workable, realistic organization for world peace—and his own simple, personal dreams for the years that he would spend after his retirement from the Presidency."

That was Roosevelt the friend, the wartime President and world figure, as Sherwood paid public tribute to him. His private salute is given in the pencil memorandum, written by Sherwood to himself, which I came across in his files, tucked away in the *New York Times* account of Roosevelt's death and funeral.

It is as though for years I had been a stoker for a gigantic powerhouse which gave power and heat and light—not only for today, but for all time to come. Some of the coal I had mined myself—some had been given to me by others, as when some stranger handed me a lump (knowing the privilege of my stoker's position) and said, "Here—I think this will be useful in that mighty furnace."

And then, suddenly, the powerhouse is gone. It is no more. It is in a grave in a rose garden in Hyde Park. It is as static, as impotent, as cold as any other grave.

This is an inexpressibly sad moment in my life as a worker.

There is no cause for worry because of the fact that no one from now on will offer me lumps of coal to put into that great furnace. They will find other furnaces that require stoking.

But what will I do with my own coal, granted that I have any left?

Part Two

THERE SHALL BE
NO NIGHT

by

Robert E. Sherwood

As the previous pages indicate, there were various versions of There Shall Be No Night. *Sherwood continued to revise the play—even after it went into actual production. As far as can be ascertained, the following text is the final authorized version.*

THIS PLAY IS DEDICATED

WITH MY LOVE TO MY WIFE

MADELINE

There Shall Be No Night was produced and presented by the Playwrights' Company—Maxwell Anderson, S. N. Behrman, Elmer Rice, Robert E. Sherwood—and the Theatre Guild—for the first time at the Opera House in Providence on March 29, 1940, with the following cast:

DR. KAARLO VALKONEN..............Alfred Lunt

MIRANDA VALKONEN...............Lynn Fontanne

DAVE CORWEEN.....................Richard Whorf

UNCLE WALDEMAR.................Sydney Greenstreet

GUS SHUMAN.....................Brooks West

ERIK VALKONEN...................Montgomery Clift

KAATRI ALQUIST..................Elisabeth Fraser

DR. ZIEMSSEN....................Maurice Colbourne

MAJOR RUTKOWSKI...............Edward Raquello

JOE BURNETT.....................Charles Ansley

BEN GICHNER....................Thomas Gomez

FRANK OLMSTEAD.................William Le Massena

SERGEANT GOSDEN................Claude Horton

LEMPI...........................Phyllis Thaxter

ILMA...........................Charva Chester

CAMERA MAN.....................Ralph Nelson

CAMERA MAN.....................Robert Downing

Staged by Alfred Lunt.

Settings designed by Richard Whorf.

SCENES

PREFACE

After the first performance of *There Shall Be No Night* in Providence on March 29, 1940, a young man, a stranger, came up to me and said, "You certainly have changed your point of view since *Idiot's Delight*." There was a distinct note of accusation in his voice. This was the first of many similar and many less temperate accusations which this play has provoked. Having identified myself time and again in the past as a pacifist, I had now become a "Warmonger."

It is a strange fact that many people who can bear with equanimity all sorts of assaults upon their moral character or their personal habits are goaded to indignant counter-attack when they are charged with inconsistency. "I don't mind being called a black-hearted villain, an enemy of society. In fact, I might even be flattered by such distinction. But—by God—I'll fight any man who dares to imply that I have been untrue to myself.''

Therefore, I wish to preface this play with a review of the development of my own point of view, as it has been expressed in other plays. I want to say that *There Shall Be No Night* is not a denial of *Idiot's Delight*: it is a sequel. I realize that there is an appreciable difference between what I have written and what I have tried to write. But I shall deal in this Preface with my motives, and the nature of the experience which impelled them.

As a common soldier in the Canadian army in the First World War, in training camps, in the line, in hospitals, and in clinks, I was mixed in with men from all over the British Empire and the United States. In one hospital the occupant of the bed on one side of mine was an Australian who had been horribly burned by liquid fire in the crater at Loos three years before. In the bed on the other side of mine was a South African Jew; a machine-gun bullet had lodged in the base of his spine and he knew he would never walk again. It was a great surprise to me to discover that these two men, and all other men whom I got to know well, thought and talked and acted and reacted just about as I did. What was so surprising about it was the revelation of the narrowness and shallowness of my own mind. I had been brought up to believe that because I was a 100 per cent American —and a Harvard man, at that—I was superior.

At the age of twenty-two my career as a soldier was ended—for all time, as I then hopefully believed. I became a veteran, and as such recaptured a certain sense of superiority. (That didn't last long, either. Never was there a baser deception than the famous recruiting poster which showed a cute little girl pointing a chubby finger at her father and asking, "Daddy—what did YOU do in the Great War?" As things have turned out, when the children of my generation point the finger at us the one word that follows it is "Sucker!") I took with me out of the army certain convictions, which have stayed with me and which all the dreadful events of the past twenty years have served only to strengthen.

I became internationally minded—and in the opinion of the apostles of isolationism, the word "international-ist" is synonymous with "warmonger." I believed that war was a hideous injustice and that no man had the right to call himself civilized as long as he admitted that another world war could conceivably be justifiable. I believed that the beginning of the elimination of war was the elimination of nationalism, the chauvinistic concept of patriotism. And I believed that the beginning of the elimination of nationalism was in some form of union of the English-speaking peoples who were already united by the advantages of a common language, common traditions of freedom, common ethics, and a common desire for peace.

I was instinctively enthusiastic about the scheme for a League of Nations. I wanted to believe that there would be some medium for expressing the good will that I shared with the scalded Australian and the paralyzed South African Jew. But, in 1919, I was convinced of the futility of the League by the writings of George Harvey and other Wilson-haters. I became a rabid opponent of the League—which means that whenever I engaged in a discussion of the major political issues in some speak-easy I would say, "The League won't work because it's impractical. I agree absolutely with Senator Henry Cabot Lodge that Article XVI stinks!" I had a very hazy idea of what Article XVI actually provided for, but I was young and free again and it was much more fun to be a critic than an adherent.

In 1920, I confess with deep shame, my first vote as an American citizen was cast for Warren G. Harding. Thus, I did my bit in the great betrayal. I voted for the proposition that all the American soldiers who had given their lives in the Great War had died in vain. And what I and all other Americans got from Harding's victory was a decade of hypocrisy, corruption, crime, glorification of greed and depravity, to be followed logically by a decade of ascendant Hitlerism.

In 1926 I wrote my first play. My main reason for doing so was that I was about to be thirty years old, and I had read somewhere—I think it was in F.P.A.'s column— that all young newspapermen promise themselves that they will write that play or that novel before they're thirty and then the next thing they know they're forty and still promising. I didn't have time for a novel. When I wrote *The Road to Rome* I didn't know what sort of playwright I might be, provided I might be a playwright at all. So I tried in it every style of dramaturgy—high comedy, low comedy, melodrama, romance (both sacred and profane), hard-boiled realism, beautiful writing— and, of course, I inserted a "message." That message was that I was opposed to war. But any one who remembers *The Road to Rome* remembers it principally for one line, which came near the end of the play. Hannibal, the Carthaginian conqueror, having spent a night with Amytis, the wife of the Roman dictator, Fabius Maximus, has been persuaded by that pleasant experience to spare Rome from destruction. When Hannibal is about to retreat from the Eternal City, the following dialogue occurs:

HANNIBAL.
Fabius, I wish happiness and prosperity to you, your wife, and your sons.

FABIUS.
Thank you—but I have no sons.

HANNIBAL.
You may have . . .

After *The Road to Rome* I made several unsuccessful attempts to repeat the same formula: "a modern comedy in ancient dress." Chief of these was a play (unproduced) called *Marching as to War*. The scene of this was England in the reign of Richard the Lion-hearted and the hero of it was a conscientious objector who refused to go on the Crusade.

In October, 1929—while Prime Minister Ramsay Mac-Donald was visiting President Herbert Hoover, offering "Faith, Hope and Parity," and Wall Street was just getting ready to crash—I tried another kind of play, *Waterloo Bridge,* which was written from my own observations of blacked out, hungry London in 1917. The most important speech in this was spoken by a Canadian soldier. He has just emerged from hospital—an air-raid is going on—and his girl tells him he must go back to France and fight the war. He says:

"Yes—fight the war. What's the war, anyway? It's that guy up there in his aeroplane. What do I care about him and his bombs? What do I care who he is, or what he does, or what happens to him? That war's over for me. What I've got to fight is the whole dirty world. That's the enemy that's against you and me . . ."

Waterloo Bridge was almost good. But it was incoherent. Two years after it, I wrote *Reunion in Vienna*. I went into this play with what seemed to me an important if not strikingly original idea—science hoist with its own petard—and came out with a gay, romantic comedy. But in the Preface to that play I came closer than I ever had before to a statement of what I was trying to think and write. I quote at length from this Preface, because it has a considerable bearing on all that I have written since then:

> This play is another demonstration of the escape mechanism in operation.
>
> There is no form of mechanism more popular or in more general use in this obstreperously technological period—which is a sufficient indication of the spirit of moral defeatism that now prevails. It is a spirit, or want of spirit, that can truthfully be said to be new in the world—for the reason that in no previous historic emergency has the common man enjoyed the dubious advantages of consciousness. However unwillingly, he is now able to realize that his generation has the ill-luck to occupy the limbo-like interlude between one age and another. Looking about him, he sees a shell-torn No Man's Land, filled with barbed-wire entanglements and stench and uncertainty. If it is not actual chaos, it is a convincing counterfeit thereof. Before him is black doubt, punctured by brief flashes of ominous light, whose revelations are not comforting. Behind him is nothing but the ghastly wreckage of burned bridges.
>
> In his desperation, which he assures himself is essentially comic, he casts about for weapons of defense. The old minds offer him Superstition, but it is a stringless bow, impotent in its obsolescence. The new minds offer him Rationalism, but

it is a boomerang. He must devise pitiful defenses of his own, like a soldier who spreads a sheet of wrapping paper over his bivouac to keep out the airplane bombs. In Europe, this manifests itself in the heroic but anachronistic attempt to re-create the illusions of nationalism: people drugging them-selves with the comforting hope that tomorrow will be a repetition of yesterday, that the Caesars and the Tudors will return.

In America, which has had no Caesars or Tudors, nor even any Hohenzollerns or Habsburgs, the favorite weapon of de-fense against unlovely reality is a kind of half-hearted cyni-cism that is increasingly tremulous, increasingly shrill. . . .

Democracy—liberty, equality, fraternity, and the pursuit of happiness! Peace and prosperity! Emancipation by en-lightenment! All the distillations of man's maturing intelli-gence have gone sour.

The worst of it is that man had been so full of hope. He had complete confidence in the age of reason, the age of the neutralization of nature, for it was his own idea. It differed from all previous ages in this great respect: it was not caused by the movements of glaciers, the upheaval or submersion of continents, the imposition of prolonged droughts: it was the product of man's restless thought and tireless industry, planned and developed by him not in collaboration with nature but in implacable opposition to it. The reasonings of such as Roger Bacon, Copernicus, Galileo and Newton started the assault upon ignorance, and it has been carried on by countless thinkers and talkers from Voltaire and Rousseau to Shaw and Wells.

This is the career of the age of reason:

The eighteenth century knew the excitements of conception, culminating in the supreme orgasm of the French Revolution.

The nineteenth century was the period of gestation, marred by occasional symptoms of nausea and hysteria and a few dark forebodings, but generally orderly and complacent.

For the twentieth century have remained the excruciating labor pains and the discovery that the child is a monster; and as modern man looks upon it, and recalls the assurances of the omniscient obstetricians, he is sore distressed. He wishes that with his eyes he could see not, that with his ears he could not hear. But his senses are remarkably acute. . . .

Man is, for the moment, scornful of the formulae of the scientists, for he believes that it was they who got him into this mess. To hell with them, and their infallible laws, their experiments noble in motive and disastrous in result, their antiseptic Utopia, their vitamines and their lethal gases, their cosmic rays and their neuroses, all tidily encased in cellophane. To hell with them, says man, but with no relish, for he has been deprived even of faith in the potency of damnation. . . .

So man is giving loud expression to his reluctance to confront the seemingly inevitable. He is desperately cherishing the only remaining manifestation of the individualism which first distinguished him in the animal kingdom: it is the anarchistic impulse, rigorously inhibited but still alive—the impulse to be drunk and disorderly, to smash laws and ikons, to draw a mustache and beard on the Mona Lisa, to be a hurler of bombs and monkey wrenches—the impulse to be an artist and a damned fool. It was this impulse which animated Galileo in the face of Romanism and Lenin in the face of Tsarism, but the disciples of both of them are determined to exterminate it and can undoubtedly do so, with the aid of the disciples of Freud. There is no reason why the successful neutralization of nature cannot be extended to include human nature.

Man has been clinging to the hope that has been his since he was delivered from feudalism—hope that he may live a life which is, in the words of Whitman, 'copious, vehement, spiritual, bold.' He is seeing that hope destroyed by instruments of his own devising, and the reverberations of his protest are shaking his earth.

Perhaps this protest is only the last gasp of primitivism. Perhaps man feels that the traditions of his race demand of him a show of spirit before he submerges himself in the mass and that, when the little show is over, he will be glad enough to fall meekly into line. . . .

Such were my unhappy thoughts in the winter of 1931-32, the winter of deepest depression and of the Lindbergh kidnapping. It was the year before Hitler came to power.

During the next two years I wrote five plays. Four of these went right into the bureau drawer, never to reappear. The fifth, *Acropolis,* was produced in London and failed financially. It has never been done in the professional theatre in the United States. It was by all odds the best play I had written and the most positive affirmation of my own faith. It was a reaction, a rebellion against the despairing spirit of the *Reunion in Vienna* Preface, a rebellion that I have continued ever since. *Acropolis* was another historical analogy, but a legitimate one. The scene was Athens in the final years of the Periclean Age, when the triumph of Athenian democracy was being challenged by Spartan totalitarianism. It ended with some lines paraphrasing Pericles' funeral oration:

"I cannot give you any of the old words which say how fair and noble it is to die in battle. But I can give you the memory of our Commonwealth, as we have seen it and fallen in love with it, day by day. I can tell you, with truth, that the story of our Commonwealth will never die, but will live on, far away, woven into the fabric of other men's lives, in a world that is filled not with terror but with glory. . . ."

Some of these same words are in *There Shall Be No Night.*

Following *Acropolis,* I wrote *The Petrified Forest.* This was my first real attempt to write a play about my own country in my own time, to speak out directly. It contained its own Preface. In the following dialogue is the essence of this play:

SQUIER.

I don't know anything. You see—the trouble with me is, I belong to a vanishing race. I'm one of the intellectuals.

GABBY.

That means you've got brains. I can see you have.

SQUIER.

Yes—brains without purpose. Noise without sound. Shape without substance. Have you ever read *The Hollow Men?*
She shakes her head.
Don't. It's discouraging, because it's true. It refers to the intellectuals, who thought they'd conquered Nature. They damned it up, and used its waters to irrigate the wastelands. They built streamlined monstrosities to penetrate its resistance. They wrapped it up in cellophane and sold it in drugstores. They were so certain they had it subdued. And now— do you realize what it is that is causing world chaos?

GABBY.

No.

SQUIER.

Well, I'm probably the only living person who can tell you. . . . It's Nature hitting back. Not with the old weapons—floods, plagues, holocausts. We can neutralize them. She's fighting back with strange instruments called neuroses. She's deliberately afflicting mankind with the jitters. Nature is proving that she can't be beaten—not by the likes of us. She's taking the world away from the intellectuals and giving it back to the apes . . .

Some of this is also in *There Shall Be No Night.*

The Petrified Forest was a negative, inconclusive sort of play, but I have a great fondness for it because it pointed me in a new direction, and that proved to be the way I really wanted to go.

Idiot's Delight was written in 1935. It was about the outbreak of the Second World War. It was completely American in that it represented a compound of blank pessimism and desperate optimism, of chaos and jazz. It was also representative of its author. I think I can say that completely typical of me was a speech spoken by Harry Van, an itinerant, small-time showman. He is conversing with a German bacteriologist, Doctor Waldersee, who is forced by war to end his experiments on a cancer cure and devote himself henceforth to the service of his country in dealing out death. (The same problem as Doctor Valkonen's in *There Shall Be No Night*.) Harry Van tries to reassure this German victim of Nazism.

"I've remained an optimist," he says, "because I'm essentially a student of human nature. You dissect corpses and rats and similar unpleasant things. Well—it has been my job to dissect suckers! I've probed into the souls of some of the god-damnedest specimens. And what have I found? Now—don't sneer at me, Doctor—but above everything else I've found Faith! Faith in peace on earth, and good will to men—and faith that 'Muma,' the three-legged girl, really has got three legs. All my life, I've been selling phony goods to people of meagre intelligence and great faith. You'd think that would make me contemptuous of the human race, wouldn't you? But—on the contrary—it has given *me* Faith. It has made me sure that no matter how much the meek may be bulldozed or gypped—they *will* eventually inherit the earth."

Idiot's Delight was certainly an anti-war play; it was also violently anti-Fascist. In its postscript I wrote: "If people will continue to be intoxicated by the synthetic spirit of patriotism, pumped into them by megalomaniac leaders, and will continue to have faith in the 'security' provided by those lethal weapons sold to them by the armaments industry, then war is inevitable; and the world will soon resolve itself into the semblance of an ant hill, governed by commissars who owe their power to the profundity of their contempt for the individual members of their species.'' The point I was trying to make all through *Idiot's Delight* is the same point that I have tried again to make in the radio speech by Doctor Valkonen in the first scene of *There Shall Be No Night*.

Just half way between the writing of these two plays, in 1937, I wrote *Abe Lincoln in Illinois*. That was a logical development, although I wasn't aware of it at the time. It was the story of a man of peace who had to face the issue of appeasement or war. He faced it. His ''House Divided'' speech made him a national figure and the candidate of the party which was determined to end slavery. Douglas accused Lincoln of ''inflammatory persuasion,'' of ''stimulating the passions of men to violence,'' but Lincoln did not retreat from the uncompromising stand which, after years of doubt and hesitancy, he had chosen to take. A few days after his inauguration as President, he was confronted with the grave situation of Fort Sumter. He asked his cabinet whether in their opinion he should send relief to Fort Sumter. The cabinet voted eight to one against doing so, on the ground that such action would most certainly mean war. Lincoln, on his own authority, ordered the relief to be sent to Fort Sumter. It did mean war—and for Lincoln it meant four years of anguish and then violent death. But it saved the Union.

The development of Lincoln's attitude in the years before the Civil War paralleled the development of the attitude of the whole American people in the years before 1940. Lincoln knew that slavery was an evil, but considered war a greater evil. He served in Congress for one term during the Mexican War, and in 1848 he denounced that war, calling it a land grab, as indeed it was. His "unpatriotic" stand at this time caused a newspaper in his own home state to denounce him as "a second Benedict Arnold."

Lincoln then believed that, if the Southern States wanted slavery, they were perfectly free to have slavery. He didn't say much about this vital issue; but when he talked at all, he expressed his disapproval of the rabble-rousing agitations of the Abolitionists. This was the liberal democratic point of view of "live and let live." It was the point of view of ordinary Americans—and Englishmen and Frenchmen, as well—in 1936 when they said, "If the Germans want Naziism, or the Italians Fascism, or the Russians Communism, that is their business, and not ours." (I tried to say in *Idiot's Delight* that it was everybody's business. There is no more dangerous error of foreign policy than for the government of one nation to say, "We are not concerned with the internal affairs of other nations.")

It was when Lincoln saw that the spirit of acceptance of slavery was spreading—from Missouri into Kansas and Nebraska and on across the plains and mountains to Oregon and California—it was then that he turned from an appeaser into a fighter.

While *Abe Lincoln in Illinois* was in rehearsal, in September, 1938, the Munich crisis occurred. I showed Raymond Massey a passage from Lincoln's Peoria speech, of 1854, which seemed to have a direct bearing on the current situation. We decided to incorporate this into the speech which Mr. Massey delivered so brilliantly in the debate scene.

Lincoln, in this passage, was talking of the Douglas policy of "mind your own business"—the policy of indifference to evil—the policy of appeasement. He said he "could not but hate" it. "I hate it because of the monstrous injustice of slavery itself. I hate it because it deprives our republic of its just influence in the world; enables the enemies of free institutions everywhere to taunt us as hypocrites; causes the real friends of freedom to doubt our sincerity; and especially because it forces so many good men among ourselves into an open war with the very fundamentals of civil liberty, denying the good faith of the Declaration of Independence, and insisting that there is no right principle of action but *self-interest.*"

Those words have had a profound influence on my own thinking, or attempts at thought.

After *Abe Lincoln in Illinois,* two years passed during which I had many doubts that I should ever write another play. I wanted to write about that which was uppermost in my own mind and in the minds of most other men who were still free to speak. But how could any play hope to compete or even keep up with the daily headlines and the shrieks of increasing horror heard over the radio? I said to my friend, Alexander Korda, "I wish I could write a sparkling drawing-room comedy without a suggestion of international calamity or social significance or anything else of immediate importance." He laughed and said, "Go ahead and write that comedy—and you'll find that international calamity and social significance are right there, in the drawing room.''

With the outbreak of the Second World War in 1939 I was in a frenzy of uncertainty. I knew all the arguments for keeping my own country out of the European conflict; I had uttered many of them myself, and at the top of my lungs. I had learned that the forces which had got us into war in 1917 were sympathy for the Allies and hatred of German militarism, economic involvement with the Allies, and the great national campaign for preparedness which began at Plattsburg in 1915-16. (I was there.) I believed that he that taketh up the sword is going to use it, however he may try to persuade himself, ''I do this not because of a desire to fight but because I wish to avoid fighting.'' That is why, for the twenty years which followed 1918, I was a passionate advocate of disarmament. It was a bitter moment for me when I found myself on the same side as the Big Navy enthusiasts.

All of these considerations were storming around in my mind in September, 1939, and storming with them was the conviction that Hitlerism was as great a menace to the United States as it was to any free country of Europe —that as a force it was far more formidable than most complacent people in the democracies supposed—that England and France, if we failed to help them, might crumble quickly before it and that then we should be helpless to oppose it.

Being myself so confused, I couldn't speak up with any positive conviction. I was terrified of identifying myself as a ''Warmonger.'' But my mind was settled principally by two events: the first was a speech in October by Colonel Charles A. Lindbergh, which proved that Hitlerism was already powerfully and persuasively represented in our own midst; the second was the Soviet invasion of Finland.

Like many another who hopes that he is a Liberal, I had great faith in the Soviet Union as a force for world peace. I believed it was the mightiest opponent of Fascism. The Russian aid to the Spanish Loyalists and the Chinese substantiated that belief. Even after the news of the Nazi-Soviet treaty I continued to think wishfully that Stalin was playing his own shrewd game against Fascism. But with the assault on Finland the last scales of illusion fell. I knew that this was merely part of Hitler's game of world revolution; and it was not proletarian revolution—far from it; it was a new and immeasurably more virulent form of imperialism. The Soviet government was playing the old, inhuman game of power politics with the same Machiavellian cynicism which has been Fascism's deadliest weapon against the gullible democracies. The Marxian principles of internationalism were as dead as Lenin. The Soviet warlords cared no more for the fate of the workers in the United States than they had cared for the fate of the workers in France. The sole purpose of their propaganda in the United States, as it had been in France, was to spread confusion and disunion, to weaken American resistance so that we would provide an irresistible temptation to Hitler to continue his conquests westward.

The reluctance of the United States to give help to Finland shocked me. The sentiment of our people for the Finns was obvious. Here was a decent little democracy, which had paid its debts and played no part in any of the vicious European intrigues, ruthlessly assaulted by an

overwhelmingly superior force and gallantly fighting for
its own freedom. There could be only one reason for
America's reluctance to give any help to the Finns, and
that was abject fear. And if we were in a state of abject
fear, then we had already been conquered by the masters
of the Slave states and we must surrender our birthright.

So I decided to raise my voice in protest against the
hysterical escapism, the Pontius Pilate retreat from decision, which dominated American thinking and, despite
all the warnings of the President of the United States
and the Secretary of State, pointed our foreign policy
toward suicidal isolationism. I wrote this play in January
and February, 1940, under constant pressure of the
knowledge that it might at any moment be rendered hope-
lessly out of date. As it happened, the war in Finland
ended while the play was in rehearsal. But the story of
the Finns' three months of resistance continued to be the
story of all decent, civilized people who choose to stand
up and fight for their freedom against the forces of
atavistic despotism. Shortly after the play's first opening, two more innocent countries, Denmark and Norway,
were invaded by the Nazis. Then came the invasion and
conquest of Holland, Belgium and France.

I was rather surprised, under the circumstances of
writing, that this play developed a spirit of optimism
along toward the end. But, in expressing my own essential faith, as I have tried to do herein, I couldn't very
well keep optimism out. I believe every word that Doctor
Valkonen utters in the sixth scene of *There Shall Be No
Night*. I believe that man, in his new-found consciousness,
can find the means of his redemption. We are conscious
of our past failures. We are conscious of our present

perils. We must be conscious of our limitless future opportunities. We are armed with more bitter experience, more profound knowledge, than any generations that ever were in the history of the world. If we can't use this experience and this knowledge then the human story is really finished and we can go back and achieve forgetfulness and peace in the ooze from which we ascended.

It seems to me, as this Preface is written, that Doctor Valkonen's pessimism concerning man's mechanical defenses and his optimistic faith in man himself have been justified by events. The Mannerheim and Maginot Lines have gone. But the individual human spirit still lives and resists in the tortured streets of London.

I wish to express my gratitude to my family doctor, Charles Goodman Taylor, for the advice he gave me in forming the scientific philosophy of Doctor Valkonen; to W. L. White, for his broadcasts over CBS from Finland —especially the deeply stirring one on Christmas Day, 1939—from which I gained almost all of my sketchy knowledge of the Soviet-Finnish War; to Anne Morrow Lindbergh, for an article of hers in the January, 1940, issue of the *Reader's Digest;* to my associates of the Playwrights' Company for invaluable suggestions for revisions in this hastily written play; and—for the third time in my life—to Lynn Fontanne and Alfred Lunt.

R.E.S.

September 13, 1940

THERE SHALL BE NO NIGHT

SCENE I

The scene is the living room of the Valkonen house in the suburbs of Helsinki. It is afternoon of a day early in October, 1938.

This is a nice, neat, old-fashioned house, with large windows, through which one sees a lovely view of the harbor and the islands.

The room is comfortably furnished. On the walls, surprisingly, are pictures from an American house. The most prominent is a portrait of a handsome naval officer of the 1812 era. There are a dismal portrait of a substantial magnate of the 1880's, and a number of pallid little water-colors of Louisiana scenes. There is a charcoal drawing of a wistful looking gentleman. On the piano and on the tables are many photographs of famous doctors—Pavlov, Freud, the Mayos, Carrel, etc.

Up-stage, a large door leads into the dining room.

An unseen door leads from this into the kitchen, to the right.

The main entrance, leading from the front hall, is lower right. The piano is upper left.

Near the center of the stage is a sofa, and in front of it, on a table, are a radio microphone and a telephone.

Wire connections for this equipment run out into the dining room, where there are a mixer and other equipment.

Standing at the left of this table is DR. KAARLO VALKONEN. *He is between forty-five and fifty years old— gentle, amused, vague, and now rather self-conscious. Beside him stands his wife,* MIRANDA, *who is beautiful, chic, and enjoying the whole situation intensely.* KAARLO *is a native Finn;* MIRANDA *comes from New Bedford, Massachusetts.*

In the foreground are two CAMERA MEN *with flash cameras. They are taking pictures of the Valkonens.*

Toward the right stands DAVE CORWEEN, *an American, about thirty-five years old, formerly a newspaper foreign correspondent, now a European representative of the Columbia Broadcasting System.*

FIRST CAMERA MAN.
Now—Doctor——

KAARLO.
Yes—I'm ready.

MIRANDA.
Wait a minute——
She removes KAARLO'S *glasses.*

FIRST CAMERA MAN.

Smile, please——

> *They both smile. The picture is taken. The* CAMERA MEN *bow and cross to the left.*

DAVE.

Will you both sit down, please?

> KAARLO *and* MIRANDA *sit on the sofa.*

Dr. Valkonen, would you look as though you were talking into the mike?

KAARLO.

Talking?

MIRANDA.

Just say something, Kaarlo—something thrilling and profound.

DAVE.

Say 1-2-3-4-5-6-7—anything.

MIRANDA.

And I'll look as if I were listening, fascinated.

DAVE.

> *Smiles.*

That's right, Mrs. Valkonen.

FIRST CAMERA MAN.

Ready?

> *They pose for an instant while he takes the picture. He changes negatives and takes several more pictures during* KAARLO'S *speech.*

DAVE.

Can't you think of something? We want to test the microphone.

KAARLO.

Nodding.

Yes! I can think of something.

He leans toward the microphone.

How do you do, my dear friends in America? How are you? I am well. I hope you are likewise. And do you know that the human digestive tract or alimentary canal extends for a distance of twenty-five to thirty feet, and consists of the following main parts: the mouth, pharynx, œsophagus, stomach, small intestines, cæcum, large intestines, rectum and anus? Into this canal flow the secretions of the salivary glands, liver and pancreas. Don't I speak English nicely? Yes. Thank you. Is that enough?

The CAMERA MEN *have finished and pack their equipment, preparing to leave.*

DAVE.

That was splendid, Doctor. Thank you very much.

SECOND CAMERA MAN.

Thank you, Doctor.

KAARLO.

Don't mention it, gentlemen.

MIRANDA.

Will we get copies of those pictures?

FIRST CAMERA MAN.

Oh yes, Mrs. Valkonen. We hope you will like them.

KAARLO.

Thank you.

The CAMERA MEN *bow and go out at the right.*

DAVE.

Calling toward the dining room.

How was it, Gus?

GUS *appears in the dining-room door. He is a young American radio mechanic.*

GUS.

It sounded fine. Just speak in that same natural way, Doctor.

MIRANDA *turns to* DAVE *with some alarm.*

MIRANDA.

Was that radio on when he was talking?

GUS *goes.*

DAVE.

Don't worry, Mrs. Valkonen. It was just a test. The voice went no farther than the next room.

MIRANDA.

Now, Kaarlo—when you do speak to the American people, please don't forget yourself and go through all those disgusting organs again. People don't like to be reminded of such things.

KAARLO.

But I don't know yet what I'm supposed to say. You haven't finished correcting that translation.

MIRANDA.

Rising.

I'll finish it now. Would you like a drink, Mr. Corween?

DAVE.

Not just now, thank you.

MIRANDA.

We'll all have a drink after the broadcast.

She goes out. KAARLO *has been looking at the radio apparatus.*

KAARLO.

Wonderful business, this.

DAVE.

Wonderful—and awful.

KAARLO.

More complicated than the alimentary canal, eh?

DAVE.

Perhaps. But less essential.

KAARLO.

How does my voice get from here all the way to America? Can you explain that to me?

DAVE.

No, Doctor—I can't. But I can give you the outline. The voice travels from the microphone along that wire into the next room. It goes into that box in there. That's called the mixer. From there, it goes over your own telephone line to the broadcasting station, where various things happen that I don't understand. It's then transmitted on another line under the Gulf of Finland to Geneva, where it's broadcast by short wave from the League of Nations station.

KAARLO.

Really! So that's what the League of Nations is doing!

DAVE.

Well, they've got to do something. They send your voice

to some place on Long Island, where it's transmitted to CBS in New York, and then rebroadcast from coast to coast.

KAARLO.

My word! Do you think any one will listen?

DAVE.

Laughing.

Certainly. They'll listen to all sorts of strange things on Sunday.

KAARLO.

I knew I should never have agreed to this nonsense. I'll make a fool of myself.

DAVE.

Oh, please, Doctor—I didn't mean to suggest that——

KAARLO.

I know you didn't. But I'm still sorry. My wife's relatives will be listening, and they will write to her and say, "Kaarlo sounds older." They live in New Bedford, Massachusetts. Have you ever been there?

DAVE.

I couldn't be sure.

KAARLO.

A depressing place. But good people. Terrifying—but good. All of these paintings on the wall came from the house in New Bedford. (*He points to the 1812 officer.*) There's a fine looking fellow. They must have been gayer in those days. But look at that one over there. Miranda's grandfather. Did you ever see such a brigand? That's a drawing of her father on the piano. A very sensitive face. He didn't come from New Bedford—Louisiana, I think. He painted all those water-colors—swamps, and things. Miranda loved him. He must have been very charming. But he was surely a very bad painter.

UNCLE WALDEMAR *comes in from the right. He is a moody, disenchanted old man.* KAARLO *rises and crosses to him.*

Ah, Uncle Waldemar—I was afraid you were going to be late.

KAARLO *kisses* UNCLE WALDEMAR.

This is Mr. Corween, of the American radio—my uncle Mr. Sederstrum.

DAVE.
How do you do?

UNCLE WALDEMAR.
Curtly.
How do you do?
He crosses to his easy chair at the left.

KAARLO.
If you would like to have some music with the broadcast, Uncle Waldemar will play. A great musician. He plays the organ in the Agricola Church.

UNCLE WALDEMAR.
Thank you. But I think you can do without music.

KAARLO.
Look at this machine, Uncle Waldemar.
KAARLO *goes up to the couch and points to the micro-phone.*

My voice goes in there, and then into the dining room
where it gets mixed, and then to the League of Nations,
and then all over America. They will all be listening,
because it's Sunday.

He turns to DAVE.

Will they hear me even in Minnesota?

DAVE.

Yes, Doctor. Even in Minnesota.

KAARLO.

It makes one frightened.

He sits down.

DAVE.

I know it does. I've been broadcasting for nearly a year
now, all over Europe, and I still get mike fright when I
hear that summons, "Come in, Vienna" or "Go ahead,
Prague," or wherever I happen to be.

DAVE *sits down.*

KAARLO.

You were in Prague during the crisis?

DAVE.

Yes—I just came from there—Prague and Munich.

KAARLO.

You saw all of it, there in Munich?

DAVE.

As much as we were allowed to see.

KAARLO.

When we read our papers the day after that meeting last
week—we just couldn't believe it. Something had hap-

pened that we couldn't understand. Could we, Uncle Waldemar?

UNCLE WALDEMAR.

I could. I knew it would be a disaster.

KAARLO.

Uncle Waldemar always looks on the dark side of things. There's been too much Sibelius in his life.

UNCLE WALDEMAR.

I can understand what happened at Munich because I know Germany. I've lived there—I've studied music there —I've read Goethe. He knew his own people. He stood on the heights, and he said that from his point of view all life looks like some malignant disease.

DAVE.

Well, he should see it now. I can tell you I was glad when they ordered me to come up here. You don't know what it means to be in a really free country again. To read newspapers that print *news*—to sit around cafés and hear people openly criticizing their government. Why—when I saw a girl in the street who wasn't afraid to use lipstick, I wanted to go right up and kiss her.

KAARLO.

Why didn't you? She'd have been very flattered.
Our girls here like Americans, especially those gay young college boys who come here on tours——

    MIRANDA *enters with the manuscript of the speech.* DAVE *and* KAARLO *rise.*

MIRANDA.

Here's your speech, Kaarlo.

She gives him his speech and crosses to UNCLE WALDE-MAR, *kissing him.*

Hello, Uncle Waldemar. I'm sorry I missed church today, but there's been so much excitement around——

UNCLE WALDEMAR.

It was just the same as always.

MIRANDA.

Crossing back to the table.

Kaarlo, you'd better read that speech all over to yourself first.

KAARLO.

I'll go to our room and read it to the mirror.

He goes out at the right.

DAVE.

Dr. Valkonen showed me your family portraits.

MIRANDA.

Oh, did he? Did he tell you his idea—that they represent the whole cycle of modern history? Rugged heroism—that's him—developing into ruthless materialism—that's him—

She has pointed first to the 1812 ancestor, then the 1880 one. Then she crosses to the piano and picks up the drawing.

—and then degenerating into intellectual impotence and decay—that's him.

She holds the picture fondly.

Rugged heroism—that's old great-grandfather Eustis—he fought in the navy in the war of 1812.

DAVE.

Did he?

MIRANDA.

Yes—and he lived to sail a clipper ship to California in the Gold Rush. He didn't get any gold, but he died happy. His son, my sainted grandfather—that's that one with the beard—bought his way out of the Civil War for three hundred dollars. Then he made a nice fortune selling shoddy uniforms to the army. He did even better after the war when he packed his carpet bag and went south. He married a beautiful daughter of the ruined aristocracy, and my father was the result.

She holds out the drawing.

You can see he was more New Orleans than New Bedford.

DAVE *looks at the picture over her shoulder.*

Sargent drew that. Fine drawing, isn't it?

DAVE.

Superb.

MIRANDA.

Crossing to the piano and replacing the drawing.

Father avenged the honor of the Old South. When he came into possession of the family fortune, he went systematically to work and threw it away, squandered every penny that old whiskers there had scrounged and saved. And he had a wonderful time doing it.

She gets a cigarette from a box on the piano and sits down.

He was the idol of all the head waiters in London, Paris, Monte Carlo, Vienna. He took me along with him on his travels. He used to say to me, "Mandy, this won't last forever, but while it does, we're certainly going to make the most of it."

160

DAVE.

And how did you happen to meet Dr. Valkonen?
He lights her cigarette.

UNCLE WALDEMAR.

Amused.

Are you going to put all this on the radio?

DAVE.

Oh, no! But I'd like to write something about this visit.
I try to maintain my status as a newspaper man against
the day when the public will get tired of being fed through
their ears.

MIRANDA.

Well, Kaarlo and I met in Russia in 1914. That was when
my father was coming to the end of his brilliant career
as a spendthrift. Kaarlo was a medical officer in St.
Petersburg—that's what they called it then. Oh, he was
so handsome! Thin—dark—tragic looking. I was seventeen—I'd never seen any one like him. Of course he didn't
know I was alive. Then came the war and we had to leave
for America. It was the end of the world for me. I pes-
tered him with letters regularly, and he replied—once.
After the revolution, he came to America to study, and we
met again, and after considerable effort on my part, we
were married. And that's all there is to that.

UNCLE WALDEMAR.

Then he brought her back here, his American wife, and
we asked him, "Is she rich?" and he said, "No." So we
said, "Kaarlo is a fool."

MIRANDA.

I've told you it wasn't his fault—he was too polite to
refuse.

She turns to DAVE.

All that was a long time ago. I think Uncle Waldemar has forgiven me now.

DAVE.

I hope I'll have the pleasure of meeting your son, Mrs. Valkonen.

MIRANDA.

Oh, I hope so. We're expecting him any minute. He's been away on a holiday—working. They spend all their holidays in this country working. You've never seen such energetic people.

DAVE.

I suppose your son is completely a Finn—not an American?

MIRANDA.

He can't quite make up his mind what he is. But now he has his first girl friend. She'll probably settle the matter for him.

KAARLO *comes in, carrying his speech.*

KAARLO.

Well, I've gone through this, and I must say it seems too dull, even for Sunday.

DAVE.

Looking at his watch.

It's pretty near time. I'll see if the connection is set.

DAVE *goes into the dining room.* MIRANDA *rises and goes down to* UNCLE WALDEMAR. *She arranges the shawl on his lap.* KAARLO *paces up and down, reading his speech.*

MIRANDA.

How's the rheumatism, Uncle Waldemar?

UNCLE WALDEMAR.

It's bad.

MIRANDA.

Haven't those treatments done you any good?

UNCLE WALDEMAR.

No.

MIRANDA.

Never mind. We'll be going soon to Italy for a holiday and we'll take you. That will make you well.

DAVE *returns and sits at the table, arranging his introductory speech.*

UNCLE WALDEMAR.

Yes—I know what those holidays are like, in Italy, or anywhere else. All Kaarlo does is visit lunatic asylums.

DAVE *picks up the telephone, and looks toward* GUS *in the dining room.*

GUS'S VOICE.

From the dining room.
Go ahead.

DAVE.

Into the telephone.
Hello—hello. This is Dave Corween—Dave Corween. . . . Hello, Ed. How's everything? . . . Yes—I got here this morning. Beautiful place—lovely people—and what a relief. . . . Yes!! . . . No—I don't see how there can possibly be *another* crisis this year. . . . Maybe they'll let me

come home for Christmas. . . . No—it's wonderfully quiet
up here. Sweden, too. Yes—I came through Stockholm
yesterday.

To KAARLO *and* MIRANDA.

If you'll sit down, we're about ready.

They sit on the sofa by the table.

How's the world series? . . . They did, eh. . . . Yes—I'm
watching the time. 43½—O.K.

He looks at his watch.

. . . Good-bye, Ed.

MIRANDA.

To KAARLO.

Good luck, darling—and just remember—it doesn't really
matter.

GUS'S VOICE.

From the dining room.

O.K., Dave.

DAVE.

Listen!

VOICE FROM LOUD-SPEAKER.

This is Station WABC in New York.

KAARLO.

Great God!

MIRANDA.

Did you hear that, Uncle Waldemar? It's New York!

UNCLE WALDEMAR.

I heard.

DAVE *cautions them to silence.*

VOICE FROM LOUD-SPEAKER.

We now take you to the Finnish capital. Go ahead, Helsinki.

DAVE *speaks briskly into the microphone, using notes typed on copy paper.*

DAVE.

Hello, America—this is David Corween, in Helsinki. We're bringing you the first of a series of broadcasts from Finland, Sweden and Norway, those little countries in the far north of Europe which are at peace, and intend to remain at peace. Finland is a country with a population about equal to that of Brooklyn. Like many other small nations, it achieved its freedom twenty years ago—but, unlike some of the others, it has consolidated that freedom; it has made democracy work. It has no minority problems. Its frontiers are disputed by no one. Its people are rugged, honest, self-respecting and civilized.

KAARLO *and* MIRANDA *start to speak to one another.* DAVE *signals them to be quiet and goes right on.*

I am now speaking from the home of one of Finland's most distinguished citizens, Dr. Kaarlo Valkonen, the eminent neurologist, who has received high honors in the United States, England, the Soviet Union and other nations, and has just been awarded the Nobel Prize in medicine. In announcement of this award, the directors of the Caroline Medical Institute in Stockholm stated that Dr. Valkonen has given to mankind a new understanding of the true nature and the causes of mental diseases—and I might add that those of us who have to cover the European scene these days can appreciate how much this understanding is needed.

KAARLO *is embarrassed and pained by all this; he*

keeps looking at MIRANDA, *who, however, is delighted.*
Many of you have read his book, *The Defense of Man,*
and to some of you now listening he is known personally,
as he has lived much in America, and his wife comes from
that fine old Massachusetts town, New Bedford. It gives
me great pleasure to bring you an outstanding servant of
humanity—Dr. Kaarlo Valkonen.

He moves the microphone over to KAARLO *and gestures
to him to begin.* MIRANDA *listens intently, waiting for
mishaps.*

KAARLO.

Loudly.

I never heard so much introduction.

DAVE *moves the microphone back from* KAARLO *and signals him to speak more quietly.*

To tell the truth, I think the Nobel Prize is premature.
The work I am doing will be finished by some one else
many years from now. But still—I am glad to have that
prize, as it enables us to go for a holiday in France and
Italy, and my wife will buy some new clothes in Paris.

MIRANDA.

Read what is written!

KAARLO *looks for the first time at his manuscript.*

KAARLO.

Reading.

Dr. Carrel has said, "For the first time in history, a
crumbling civilization is capable of discerning the causes
of its decay. For the first time it has at its disposal the
gigantic strength of science." And he asks, "Will we
utilize this knowledge and this power?" That's a question

far more important than speculating about the possible results of the Munich crisis. In fact, behind this question are the real causes of all the problems we now must face.

It is no doubt well known to you that insanity is increasing at an alarming rate. Indeed, the day is within sight when the few remaining sane people are put into confinement and the lunatics are at large.

Does this seem a ridiculous exaggeration? Then look about you, at the present world. You see the spectacle of a great, brilliant nation, which has contributed perhaps more than all others to scientific progress. Today, the spiritual resistance of its people has been lowered to such an extent that they are willing to discard all their moral sense, all the essential principles of justice and civilization. They glorify a theory of government which is no more than co-ordinated barbarism, under the leadership of a megalomaniac who belongs in a psychopathic ward rather than a chancellery. He seeks to create a race of moral cretins whom science has rendered strong and germless in their bodies, but feeble and servile in their minds. We now know how quickly such men can be converted into brutes.

It is all very well to say, "We will go to war and crush this mighty force. Free men will always triumph over slaves." But after the war—and on into the centuries— what then? How long will these same free men possess the spiritual strength that enables them to be free? There is a problem for science to solve—and we must begin by admitting our own mistakes.

Science has considered disease as mechanical phenomena, to be cured by mechanical means. And we have been remarkably successful. Examine the achievements in the fight against tuberculosis—typhoid—all the ancient plagues. You will see that the number of fatalities is steadily being reduced. Then look at the degenerative diseases—insanity, which is the degeneration of the brain —and cancer, which is degeneration of the tissues. These diseases are going up, almost in the same proportion as the others are going down.

Degeneration! That is the most terrifying word in the human vocabulary today. And doctors are beginning to ask, "Is there not a suspicious connection between our victories and our defeats? Are we perhaps saving children from measles and mumps that they may grow up to be neurotics and end their days in a mad-house?" Perhaps their early battles with disease toughen them. Perhaps without that essential experience, they go into maturity without having developed adequate defenses against life. What are these defenses?

St. Paul has said: "We glory in tribulation; knowing that tribulation worketh patience; and patience, experience; and experience, hope." We have been striving to eliminate tribulation, and as we have succeeded we have deprived man of his experience, and thus of his hope.

We have counted too heavily upon pills and serums to protect us from our enemies, just as we count too heavily upon vast systems of concrete fortifications and big navies to guard our frontiers. Of what avail are these artificial protections if each man lacks the power of resistance within himself?

I am not pleading for a return of measles and mumps. I am only saying that all of us have been trying too hard to find the easy way out—when man, to *be* man, needs the experience of the hard way. "There is no coming to consciousness without pain," in the words of Dr. Jung, and Science has provided no substitute for pain.

You have heard it said that the days of exploration are over—that there are no more lost continents—no more Eldorados. But I promise you that the greatest of all adventures in exploration is still before us—the exploration of man himself—his mind—his spirit—the thing we call his character—the quality which has raised him above the beasts.

"Know thyself," said the oracle. And after thousands of years, we still don't know. Can we learn before it is too late—before the process of man's degeneration has been completed and he is again a witless ape, groping his way back into the jungle?

He looks up and thrusts his manuscript away.

But why should I go on spoiling your Sunday? I want to send my greetings to New Bedford, Massachusetts. I want to send especial greetings to Minnesota, home of my dear good friends, the Mayos. Perhaps I have an especial feeling of love for Minnesota because it is so much like Finland, with many beautiful lakes, and forests of birch and pine and spruce. And I know so many fine people there, with good blood that came from Finland, and our neighboring countries of Sweden, Norway and Denmark. To them, and to all my friends in the United States of America I say, "Thank you and God bless you and good-bye."

He turns to MIRANDA *and shrugs as though to say, "I'm sorry but that was the best I could do."* MIRANDA *leans over and kisses him.*

DAVE.

Into the microphone.

Thank you, Dr. Kaarlo Valkonen. This is David Corween in Helsinki, returning you now to Columbia in New York.

KAARLO.	VOICE FROM LOUDSPEAKER.
Never will I speak to one of those damned things again.	We take you now to London. . . .

MIRANDA.

Rising.

Darling—you were wonderful! Didn't you think it was fine, Uncle Waldemar?

UNCLE WALDEMAR.

If they'll listen to that, they'll listen to anything.

DAVE.

Rising.

You were splendid, Doctor. A definite radio personality.

MIRANDA.

There!

KAARLO.

Pleased.

You really think so?

GUS *comes in from the dining room to clear the table of equipment.*

MIRANDA.

Of course he does. Now I'll go and mix the drinks.

She goes off into the dining room.

GUS.

They said it came through fine. I liked it myself. And I'm

going to get that book of yours, Doctor. I probably can't
understand it—but I'll bet it's good.

KAARLO.

Why—thank you—thank you.
  GUS *goes out into the dining room.*
What a charming man!

DAVE.

I read your book last summer when I was resting between
crises. And just the other day, when I heard I was coming
up here about the Nobel Prize, I tried to get a copy in
Munich. The bookseller assured me, solemnly, that there
could be no such book, since he had never heard of it.

KAARLO.

  Rising.
Of course, all my books are forbidden in Germany. I
should be ashamed of myself if they weren't.
  ERIK VALKONEN *comes in from the right. He is seventeen years old, but mature and calm. He is handsome
  and healthy; there is a kind of quiet humor in his expression. With him is his girl friend,* KAATRI ALQUIST,
  *young, pretty, also healthy, and quite serious. Each of
  them carries a package.* KAARLO *goes immediately to*
  ERIK, *kisses him.*
Erik! You're just too late for my broadcast. You missed
something wonderful. Hello, Kaatri, my dear.
  KAATRI *curtsies to* KAARLO. ERIK *hands* KAARLO *his package.*

ERIK.

I brought you this from Viipuri, Father.

KAARLO.

Viipurin Rinkelia! I'll have it with my coffee.

He takes KAATRI *over to* DAVE.

Let me introduce Miss Kaatri Alquist, Mr. Corween of
the American radio. And my son, Erik.

KAATRI *curtsies to* DAVE *and crosses to* UNCLE WALDEMAR.
After greeting her, UNCLE WALDEMAR *points toward the
dining room, as* ERIK *and* DAVE *shake hands.*

ERIK AND DAVE.

How do you do?

UNCLE WALDEMAR.

Mrs. Valkonen is in the dining room.

KAATRI *goes into the dining room.* ERIK *crosses to* UNCLE
WALDEMAR.

KAATRI'S VOICE.

Hello, Mrs. Valkonen.

MIRANDA'S VOICE.

Kaatri, how lovely!

ERIK.

Kissing UNCLE WALDEMAR.

Father says he was wonderful on the radio. Is that true?

UNCLE WALDEMAR.

He only said the same things you've heard a hundred
times before.

KAARLO.

Erik, take this to your mother in the dining room.

ERIK *takes the package from* KAARLO *and goes into the
dining room.*

172

ERIK.

Mother! Mother! I'm back!

MIRANDA'S VOICE.

Erik, darling! Did you have a good time?

KAARLO.

Proudly.
Fine boy, isn't he, Mr. Corween?

DAVE.

Yes, fine. It's a shame he didn't hear your broadcast. He'd
have been proud of you.

KAARLO.

Oh—I'm an object of contempt to my own son—because,
while I talk, he *acts*. He has been working on the Mannerheim Line.

DAVE.

I'm afraid I don't know where that is.

KAARLO.

It's on the isthmus—on the Russian frontier. It's our
own little Maginot.

MIRANDA.

Entering from the dining room with ERIK *and* KAATRI.
Yes, he's a definite radio personality. . . .
She puts the box of chocolates on the piano.
Now we're going to have some coffee, and some Parker
House Punch especially for you, Mr. Corween. Go and
wash, children.

KAATRI.

Yes, Mrs. Valkonen.
The two maids, ILMA *and* LEMPI, *come in from the dining*

room with tablecloth, coffee urn, and service for six which they put on the table.

ERIK.
You're not going just yet, Mr. Corween?

DAVE.
Oh, no.

ERIK.
Thank you.
He bows and goes after KAATRI *at the right.*

MIRANDA.
Sitting on the sofa.
You know, whenever any one comes home, from anywhere, there has to be a present. Kaatri brought me those chocolates, and Erik brought his father some of the bread they make in Viipuri. It's the custom of the country. Charming, isn't it?

DAVE.
Yes.
He starts to sit down.

MIRANDA.
Under her breath.
That's Uncle Waldemar's chair. Come and sit by me.

DAVE.
Sitting on the couch.
I've noticed that here—and in Sweden, too—everybody is insufferably polite. Why, yesterday, in Stockholm, my cab side-swiped another cab, so the two drivers got out and apologized to each other. It's unnatural.
UNCLE WALDEMAR *sits at the coffee table.*

174

MIRANDA.

I know. I've lived here for twenty years. I've never got used to it.

She is starting to pour the coffee.

KAARLO.

I used to think, Mr. Corween, in my ignorance, that you Americans have no national character. My wife has taught me my error. Her character is strong enough to resist all civilizing influences. And sometimes I think our son has inherited too much from her.

He sits down at the table.

MIRANDA.

That's what Kaatri thinks. Kaatri is the girl friend I was telling you about. I'm afraid she disapproves of me. I'm too shallow—too frivolous.

KAARLO.

Oh, Kaatri comes from a typically Finnish military family. Her father is a colonel and her brothers are all brought up to be fighters. Very formidable! Maybe she does disapprove of you, my dear, but in her heart she wishes she could be more like you. She wishes she could have as much fun as we do.

MIRANDA.

I'll have a good talk with her some time.

DAVE.

I'm interested in that work your son is doing.

KAARLO.

I tell him it's silly—but he won't listen.

DAVE.

It seems a sensible thing for any one to be preparing for trouble these days.

KAARLO.

Yes—eminently sensible. But they don't know how to prepare. That's the trouble. They build those concrete pillboxes, and tank traps—as if such things could save anybody when Armageddon comes.

MIRANDA.

What does it matter, darling? They enjoy doing the work.

KAARLO.

Yes—and I suppose it's good exercise.
ERIK and KAATRI come in and go to chairs at the left, by the piano.
Erik and hundreds of other students spend all their free time on the Mannerheim Line. Kaatri is there, too, with the women's organization, to do the cooking and cleaning. Oh, they have a lot of fun—and maybe a little romance in the long evenings, eh, Kaatri?

KAATRI.
She giggles, then answers soberly.
In the evening we have discussions, Dr. Valkonen.
ERIK brings KAATRI a cup of coffee.

DAVE.

And may I ask—what sort of things do you discuss?

KAATRI.

Last night we tried to arrive at some conclusions about the consequences of the Munich treaty.

176

DAVE.

I'd like to know what your conclusions were?

ERIK.

Just what you would probably hear in a similar discussion in America, Mr. Corween. We thanked heaven for the geography which puts us so far from the scene of action. We were grateful that we do not live in Czechoslovakia, or the Balkans, or even England or France.

LEMPI *enters with the punch.*

MIRANDA.

Looking around.

Ah—here it is! Here's the Parker House Punch, Mr. Corween. The old Parker House bar was the first place my father headed for after the reading of the will. I can't cook anything—but I can make the best rum punch and eggnog too. If you're ever here on New Year's Day, I'll give you some eggnog.

DAVE.

I shall not forget that invitation.

He is happy to be in the midst of such an untroubled, harmonious family.

ERIK.

You came all the way here just to have my father broadcast?

KAARLO.

You see?

DAVE.

I'm ordered to travel around Scandinavia and pick up as many features as I can.

MIRANDA.

I think we should drink a toast—to our benefactor, the late Alfred Nobel.

They all rise.

KAARLO.

That's it—Nobel!

KAARLO AND MIRANDA.

God bless him!

ERIK.

The dynamite king.

MIRANDA.

Hush, Erik. That's not in good taste.

UNCLE WALDEMAR *crosses and sits at the piano. The others resume their seats.*

KAARLO.

As for me, I don't care where the money came from. Two million marks—forty thousand dollars.

MIRANDA.

Reverting to New England.

To say nothing of the solid gold medal.

KAARLO.

To think I should see that much in a lifetime, let alone all at once.

DAVE.

To ERIK.

What are you studying?

ERIK.

Economics—sociology.

KAARLO.

And skiing. He can't make up his mind whether he wants to be another Karl Marx, or another Olympic champion.

DAVE.

Have you been much in the Soviet Union?

ERIK.

Oh, yes. We lived there when Father was working with Pavlov.

DAVE.

And you really believe they might invade this country?

ERIK.

If there were counterrevolution in Russia, anything might happen. Or the Nazis might come that way. We have to be prepared.

MIRANDA.

Erik, open the chocolates. Uncle Waldemar, play something. Play something gay. This is a celebration.

UNCLE WALDEMAR.

I don't feel gay.

MIRANDA.

Then drink this rum punch quickly and have a few more, and you'll forget your rheumatism.

She takes him a glass of punch.

DAVE.

Of course, the Nazis have been highly successful in terrifying people of the Bolshevik menace. But all the times I've been in Moscow, I've never seen anything but a passionate desire to be let alone, in peace.

UNCLE WALDEMAR *starts to play a particularly gloomy selection by Sibelius.*

KAARLO.

Certainly. I know the Russians. I was a medical officer in their army and I was with them in prison camp in Germany all through 1916. And during the revolution I was right there in Leningrad on the staff of the Strelka Hospital. I treated Lenin for a sore throat! And I can tell you about these Russians: they love to plot—but they don't love to fight. And the reason they don't love to fight is that they're a little like the Italians—they're too charming—they really don't know how to hate.

During the foregoing speech the doorbell has been heard, faintly, and LEMPI *has crossed to the right and gone out.*

MIRANDA.

Uncle Waldemar, what is that you're playing?

UNCLE WALDEMAR.

Sibelius.

MIRANDA.

Oh, darling, can't you play something a little less solemn?

LEMPI *returns and hands* MIRANDA *a card on a silver plate.* UNCLE WALDEMAR *stops playing.*

What is it? Oh, it's Dr. Ziemssen. Tell him to come in.

LEMPI *goes out.*

KAARLO.

Rising.

Dr. Ziemssen is a neighbor of ours.

DR. ZIEMSSEN *comes in. He is a mild, scholarly, correct*

German of thirty-five or forty. KAARLO *meets him at the door.*

Come in, Dr. Ziemssen. I'm delighted to see you.

ZEIMSSEN.
Shaking KAARLO's *hand.*
Herr Doktor.

ZIEMSSEN *goes to* MIRANDA, *who rises and holds out her hand.* ZIEMSSEN *kisses it.*

MIRANDA.
How do you do, Dr. Ziemssen?

ZIEMSSEN.
Frau Valkonen.

MIRANDA.
You know Miss Alquist—and my family.

ZIEMSSEN.
Bowing to each.
Fräulein—Herr Sederstrum—Erik.

KAARLO.
And may I introduce Mr. Corween of the American radio, Dr. Ziemssen.

ZIEMSSEN.
Mr. Corween! I have heard a great deal of you.

DAVE.
Sitting.
Well—that's unusual.

KAARLO.
Please——
Indicating a chair to ZIEMSSEN.

Dr. Ziemssen is the German Consul General. He has heard of everybody.

KAARLO *sits down.*

ZIEMSSEN.
Smiles.
Only the important people. I walked over, Herr Doktor, because I just this minute talked to Berlin on the telephone and they said they had heard your broadcast. They said it came through excellently and was highly entertaining.

DAVE.
It was broadcast in Germany?

ZIEMSSEN.
Oh, no. But it was heard at the government shortwave station.

KAARLO.
Good God! I seem to remember that I said some things that were not for your government to hear.

ZIEMSSEN.
Have no worries on that score, Herr Doktor. We are well accustomed to hearing the worst about ourselves. We have heard you frequently, Mr. Corween.

KAARLO.
Don't be frightened by Dr. Ziemssen. He was an anthropologist before he became a diplomat. He is very broadminded.

MIRANDA.
Will you have some American punch, Dr. Ziemssen?

ZIEMSSEN.

Thank you, no.

KAARLO.

Then have some coffee and I'll have another cup too—and some of that Viipurin Rinkelia that Erik brought.

ZIEMSSEN.

Viipurin Rinkelia!
He turns to ERIK.
Erik—is the work getting on well?

ERIK.

It seems to be. Of course I see only a small part of it.

ZIEMSSEN.

The Finnish defenses are magnificent. No one will dare to challenge them.

ERIK.

The Czechs had fine defenses, too.

ZIEMSSEN.

Ah, but you are more intelligent than the Czechs. You have no Allies—to betray you!
He laughs at that pleasantry.
How do you feel about that, Mr. Corween? You were at Munich.

DAVE.

I'm afraid I have no feeling about anything.

MIRANDA.

Then have some more punch, Mr. Corween.

DAVE.

Laughs.
No, thank you.

To ZIEMSSEN.

If you had asked me that question a few years ago—if you had asked me any questions of cosmic significance—I could have answered without a moment's hesitation. I was the youngest genius ever to be given a by-line in the Chicago *Daily News*. I was on intimate terms with both God and Mammon. The wisdom of the ages was set before me, on the halfshell. All I had to do was add horseradish and eat.

ZIEMSSEN.

Smiles.

You have become a little less confident in recent years?

DAVE.

Well, since then I have been de-educated, if there is such a word. I've covered Manchukuo, Ethiopia, Spain, China, Austria, Czechoslovakia. And all I can say is—I'm bewildered. But I suspect, Dr. Valkonen, that when you say the human race is in danger of going insane, you're not so much a prophet of future doom as a reporter of current fact.

He becomes conscious of the fact that he is holding the floor. He smiles.

I seem to be sounding off. That punch is powerful.

MIRANDA.

Good! Then have some more and tell us what it was like in Ethiopia.

DAVE.

Thank you. I mustn't. I must try to find out what it's like here.

To ERIK.

Do you suppose I could get permission to visit those defenses you're working on?

ERIK.

I should think so. Planes from Leningrad are flying over that region all the time, so I don't believe there's much secrecy.

DAVE.

I must try to get there. There might be material for a broadcast.

KAARLO.

If there's anything I can do—any letters of introduction?

DAVE.

Rising.

Oh, no, thank you. I'm trained to push in anywhere. Thank you very much, Mrs. Valkonen. You've been very kind. . . .

MIRANDA.

Shaking hands with him.

And you've been very nice. I hope you'll come and see us again.

DAVE.

I'll probably be back some time.

He crosses to shake hands with ERIK.

Certainly in 1940 for the Olympic games. Good-bye, Mr. Valkonen.

ERIK.

Good-bye, Mr. Corween.

DAVE.

To each in turn.

Good-bye, Miss Alquist.

To UNCLE WALDEMAR.

Good-bye, sir—please don't get up.

To ZIEMSSEN.

Good-bye, sir.

He crosses to KAARLO.

Good-bye, Doctor——

KAARLO.

Oh, I'll see you to the door.

They go out at the right. MIRANDA, KAATRI, *and* ZIEMS-
SEN *sit.*

MIRANDA.

Do you like him, Erik? He's nice, isn't he?

ERIK.

Yes. I wish I could do work like that. To be able to wander
all over the earth—and see things—without being a part
of them.

KAATRI *darts a worried look at* ERIK. *She knows he is
now talking with his mother's voice.*

KAATRI.

With surprising vehemence.

I'd hate such a life!

MIRANDA.

Why, Kaatri?

KAATRI.

When you see too much of the world it makes you cynical.
I'd never want to be that.

MIRANDA.

I shouldn't either. But I've traveled all over and it hasn't made me cynical. Perhaps that's because I'm just plain stupid.

ZIEMSSEN.

Ah no, Frau Valkonen. It is only because you are an American.

ERIK.

A journalist like Mr. Corween has the opportunity to see the *truth*. Maybe the ultimate truth is the ultimate futility——

MIRANDA.
Laughing at this.
Oh, dear. That boy really should have a beard.

ERIK.

Even so—I'd like to know the truth about the world. All of it!
UNCLE WALDEMAR *starts to play a gay tune.*

MIRANDA.

Kaatri, the next time we go to America, I'll ask your father and mother if you can go with us. Would you like that?

KAATRI.

Oh, I think I should love that!
KAARLO *returns and sits beside* MIRANDA.

KAARLO.

I hope some of your relatives will send us a cable so we'll know how I really sounded.

MIRANDA.

Again reverting to New England.

If I know New Bedford, they'll send a postcard. . . .

What's that you're playing now, Uncle Waldemar?

UNCLE WALDEMAR *doesn't hear. She turns to* DR. ZIEMSSEN.

What is that?

ZIEMSSEN.

Listening, appreciatively.

I believe that is Merikantor's "Tolari Ja Huotari," isn't it?

He listens for a moment.

Yes—a delightful little Finnish folk song.

UNCLE WALDEMAR *continues to play, with tinkling variations on the theme.*

MIRANDA.

Oh—I love that.

She pats KAARLO's *hand. They listen silently, happily to the music.*

CURTAIN

SCENE 11

The same. An evening late in November, 1939.
KAATRI *is sitting on the couch, looking toward* ERIK, *who is at the window by the piano, looking out.* KAATRI *is crocheting.*

KAATRI.
What are you looking at, Erik?

ERIK.
Who obviously has to think for an instant before answering this question.
I'm looking at the stars.

KAATRI.
Oh.

ERIK.
There are millions of them. They're so bright you can see them reflected on the snow.

KAATRI.

I know why you're looking out the window, Erik. Many people are looking out of their windows tonight—watching for the bombers.

ERIK.

Turning from the window.
Now, Kaatri! There are no bombers coming here.

KAATRI.

That's what they said in Poland. I'm sure they kept telling themselves, "The bombers won't come. Something will happen. There'll be another Munich. There'll be a revolution in Germany. The United States will forbid Europe to have a war. *Something* is sure to happen to prevent the bombers from coming to Poland." But they did come.

ERIK.

They were Nazis.

KAATRI.

The Russians went into Poland, too.

ERIK.

Yes, and why not? The Nazis had done the work.
He comes over and sits near her.
All the Russians had to do was march in and take all that territory at no cost to themselves. But—they know perfectly well if they attack us it would mean betrayal of the revolution! The suffering they might inflict on us would be insignificant compared to the murder of their own honor.

KAATRI.

Honor!

ERIK.

That's what my father says, and he knows them.

KAATRI.

Putting down her crocheting.

I don't believe they ever had any honor—Tsarists or Bolshevists either. My father knows them, too. That's why he has spent his life preparing to fight them when they invade our country.

ERIK.

Laughs.

Oh—Kaatri—don't let's sit here telling each other what our fathers say. We're old enough to make up our own minds, aren't we?

KAATRI.

I don't know, Erik.

ERIK.

You've made up your mind that we're going to be married, haven't you?

KAATRI.

Yes.

She laughs, shyly.

But—that's different.

ERIK.

I'm glad it *is* different. The trouble with old people is— they remember too much—old wars, old hates. They can't get those things out of their minds. But we have no such memories. We're free of such ugly things. If there's going to be a better future, we're the ones who are going to make it.

191

He takes her hands.

Kaatri——

KAATRI.

Yes, Erik?

ERIK.

Next summer I'll stop being a student. I'll be a worker!
And you and I will be married.

KAATRI.

Thrilled.

What will we live on, Erik?

ERIK.

Heroically.

On what I make. It won't be much—but it will be enough.
I'll be your man—and you'll be my woman.

They both draw apart, laugh, and then they kiss.

KAATRI.

We'll have a wonderful wedding, won't we, Erik?

ERIK.

Yes—I suppose our families will insist on that.

They are still in each other's arms.

KAATRI.

It will be in the Agricola Church, and there'll be lots of
flowers.

ERIK.

Your father will be looking stern and magnificent in his
colonel's uniform. And my father, in his black coat, looking bored. And Mother behaving like a grand duchess, and
Uncle Waldemar playing da-da-de-dum. . . .

He hums a bar of the Wedding March.

And then we'll escape from all of them, and go home, and have several children.

KAATRI.

Erik!

They both laugh happily and kiss each other again.

ERIK.

Oh, Kaatri! We'll be happy people, you and I. That's all that matters, isn't it, dearest?

KAATRI.

Yes.

Suddenly the happiness fades from her face.

No! It isn't all the matters!

ERIK.

What else is there?

KAATRI.

Looking away from him, but still holding him close.

There's *now*. . . . There's this. . . . There may be war. Next summer may never come to us.

ERIK.

I tell you—we don't have to think about those things. We're young, and we're free. We have only our own love, for each other.

UNCLE WALDEMAR *comes in. He carries a newspaper. He looks at them. They break apart guiltily, rise, and confront him with great embarrassment.*

Oh, please forgive me, Uncle Waldemar. We were——

UNCLE WALDEMAR.

Yes.

ERIK.

We were only——

UNCLE WALDEMAR

I saw what you were doing. I'm sorry to have interrupted.
He kisses KAATRI, *then* ERIK, *and crosses to the piano.*
KAATRI *sits down again.*
But there's some news here.

ERIK.

What is it?

UNCLE WALDEMAR.

It may be good. Our government has received a message
from the United States government, from Washington.
They also sent the same message to Moscow.
He comes close to them.
It's offering their good offices to settle the Soviet-Finnish
dispute. That's what they call it—the dispute. Here's
what they say.
As he starts to read, ERIK *sits on the sofa beside* KAATRI.
"We would view with extreme regret any extension of the
present area of war and the consequent further deteriora-
tion of international relations." That's what they say in
Washington.

KAATRI.

Who is holding ERIK's *hand.*
Do you suppose the Russians will listen to that?

ERIK.

Of course they'll listen.

KAATRI.

Erik believes they won't attack us. What do you believe,
Uncle Waldemar?

UNCLE WALDEMAR.

I know they *will!*

KAATRI.

To ERIK.

There!

UNCLE WALDEMAR.

Do you know what the press in Moscow is saying about us? We're "that Finnish scum"—we're "bourgeois bandits"—"tools of British imperialism"—"Fascist assassins."

He crosses to the left and flings the newspaper onto the piano.

Those words are the advance guard of the Red Army!

ERIK.

My father doesn't agree with you.

UNCLE WALDEMAR.

And what does *he* know about it?

ERIK.

As much as anyone could. He understands the Russians. He was the good friend of Pavlov and Gorki, and even Lenin himself.

UNCLE WALDEMAR.

All those gentlemen you mention are dead. And the revolution—that's dead, too. It's embalmed and exposed in a glass coffin in front of the Kremlin. It is respected—but dead. Now comes the true disintegration—the end of the world. Your father said—men might become again like apes, groping their way back into the jungle. Well—it has come to pass. Men are groping their way through the night. The lights are out in Berlin, Paris, London. And in Warsaw, they crawl through the ruins like rats. It will be the same here. This is war in the jungle, and the winner will be crowned "King of Beasts."

MIRANDA *comes in from the right, looking very smart in her furs and her Paris hat.* ERIK *and* KAATRI *rise.*

ERIK.
Hello, Mother. Where's Father?

MIRANDA.
Taking off her hat and coat.
He's at the laboratory.
She puts her wraps on a chair at the right.
I went there to try to make him come home. He had a lot of dogs there—there must have been thirty or forty of them—all barking and howling. I asked him what he was doing with all those dogs, but he told me to go away.
She kisses KAATRI.
Kaatri—are your mother and father well?

KAATRI.
My mother is well, thank you. My father is with the army in the north.

MIRANDA.
But he'll surely be home for Christmas?

KAATRI.
Oh, yes, Mrs. Valkonen—we hope so.
MIRANDA *has come up to* ERIK. *She kisses him.*

UNCLE WALDEMAR.
I have to go to the church and practice. There's to be a great service this evening—prayers for peace.

196

MIRANDA.

Sitting down on the sofa.

I know.

UNCLE WALDEMAR.

The President will be there and the Cabinet and the leaders of all parties.

He starts to cross toward the door at the right.

Tonight—prayers. Tomorrow—guns.

He goes out. There is a moment of constrained silence.

MIRANDA.

I stopped in at the American Legation on my way home and saw Mr. Walsh. I wanted to find out if he had any news. He told me that the State Department has ordered all Americans to leave Finland at once. He was very guarded in his choice of words—but he seems to think that things are rather serious.

ERIK.

So does Uncle Waldemar. But that doesn't mean anything. The American government—all governments—are being pulverized with fear by this Soviet propaganda.

He picks up the paper from the piano.

They want to pulverize us, too, so that we'll give them what they want without a struggle. It's all bluff—it's all an imitation of the Nazis.

KAATRI.

But when the bluff doesn't work, suppose they go on imitating the Nazis—suppose they do attack?

MIRANDA *looks from* KAATRI *to* ERIK, *awaiting his reply.*

ERIK.

Without emotion.

Then—we'll have to fight—that's all.

MIRANDA.

But—how can we fight?

ERIK.

To the best of our ability.

MIRANDA.

And how long will that last?

ERIK.

A few days—a few weeks—I don't know.
He is looking out the window.

MIRANDA.

Erik—*Erik!*
He turns to her.
Would *you* fight?

ERIK.

Of course I would. Everybody would!

MIRANDA.

Why? What good would that do?

ERIK.

It would prove that this country has a right to live.

MIRANDA.

And who will derive any benefit from that proof? Are
you anxious to die just to get applause from the civilized
world—applause and probably nothing else? The Czechs
are fine, brave people—but they didn't offer any resistance to the Germans.

ERIK.

They couldn't. Their resistance was stolen from them at
Munich.

MIRANDA.

Even so—they're better off now than the Poles, who did resist.

ERIK.

That doesn't affect my feeling. I only know that if any one is going to take my freedom from me, he's going to have to pay for it.

MIRANDA.

Now you're talking like a boy scout.

ERIK.

I'm your son, Mother. I have the same blood in me that you have—the blood of that gentleman up there.
He points to the portrait of great-grandfather Eustis.
He fought pirates in the Mediterranean. He fought with Jackson at New Orleans.

MIRANDA.

Yes—and when he died, in honored old age, they had.to pass the hat around among the neighbors to get enough to bury him. . . .
Pointing to the portrait of her grandfather.
Whereas that unselfish hero who paid another man to take his place in the conscript army—when he died—the whole town turned out—the Chamber of Commerce, the Republican Club, the Knights of Pythias—all paying tribute to the memory of a good, substantial citizen. If you have to look to your ancestry for guidance, look to him. He was no hero. He was a despicable, slimy cheat. But he did very well. . . . You say some one will have to pay for your freedom. But who will receive the payment? Not you, when you're dead.

KAATRI.

Fiercely.

Don't listen to her, Erik! Don't listen to her!

MIRANDA.

Amiably.

Why shouldn't he listen to me, Kaatri?

KAATRI.

With too much vehemence.

Because you're an American! You don't understand.

MIRANDA.

Patiently.

I understand one thing, Kaatri. Erik is my son. I want
to save his life.

KAATRI.

What good is his life if it has to be spent in slavery?

To ERIK.

And that's what it would be if he gave in to them. Slavery
for you—for all of us. Oh, I know that you Americans
don't like to think of such terrible things.

ERIK.

Kaatri! You mustn't say that——

MIRANDA.

Gently.

You may say what you please about me, Kaatri. But you
can't say it about Erik. He's as loyal as you are. He was
born in this house, as his father was before him.

KAATRI.

Dr. Valkonen is like you. He doesn't really belong to this
country. He is a great scientist. He has an international
mind.

MIRANDA.

And is that a bad thing?

KAATRI.

Oh, no—it's a good thing—a noble thing. But for Erik—
it would be weakness. I'm afraid for Erik—afraid that
he belongs more to America than he does to us. Oh—I
don't want to be rude, Mrs. Valkonen—to you or your
country. But wo're desperate people now. All the men in
my family—my father, my brothers—they're all in the
army now, on the frontier. It's the same with all families,
rich and poor, men and women. All our lives we've had
to be ready to fight, for everything we are, everything
we believe in. Oh, I know—it's hard for you to understand that—or to see the *need* for it that is in our souls.

ERIK.

Kaatri! Of course Mother can understand! Americans
fought for that same thing—for the same reason—the
same need, that was in their souls. It was Americans who
taught the whole world that it was *worth* fighting for!

KAATRI.

Yes. But—it's just as Dr. Valkonen says. When life becomes too easy for people, something changes in their
character, something is lost. Americans now are too
lucky.

She looks straight at MIRANDA.

In your blood is the water of those oceans that have made
your country safe. But—don't try to persuade Erik that
life here is as easy as it is in America.

She is speaking passionately, desperately.

He's a Finn, and the time has come when he must behave
like one.

ERIK.

Kaatri—my dearest—

Crossing behind the sofa, he puts a hand on KAATRI'S
right shoulder. She buries her head against him.

Don't—don't cry.

The word "dearest" makes an emphatic impression on
MIRANDA. *She stares at them.*

MIRANDA.

Kaatri—Kaatri—are you and Erik really in love with
each other?

ERIK.

Mother!

MIRANDA.

Darling, I started to talk to you as though you were still
a child—and I wanted first to reason with you—and then
if that failed, I would *forbid* you to throw your life away
for a lost cause. And then Kaatri spoke up, and you called
her "dearest," and that one word stopped me short. I
asked Kaatri that question because I thought the answer
might help me to understand this strange, new fact—that
you're not my son any more. You're a man. . . . Of course,
you don't have to answer.

ERIK.

His hand on KAATRI'S *shoulder.*

We do love each other. We are going to be married.

MIRANDA.

After a pause, kisses KAATRI.

Erik—Kaatri—I'm glad! I'm glad.

KAARLO'S VOICE.

From off-stage, right.

Erik!

ERIK *goes to the door.*

Erik! You know those litters of puppies that I separated
—eight litters?

ERIK.

Yes, Father.

KAARLO.

Entering, he throws an arm across ERIK'S *shoulders
and leads him as he talks.*

The dogs have just come back from Rovaniemi—the ones
I sent up there last year. The most wonderful results.
I've tested them in every way. Out of thirty-one dogs,
seven are definitely——

MIRANDA.

Breaking in.

Kaarlo! Kaarlo!

KAARLO.

Yes, my dear.

He slips out of his coat. To ERIK.

Take this.

To MIRANDA.

I want to apologize for being a little bit irritable when
you came into the laboratory—but I was excited. Those
dogs . . .

MIRANDA.

Never mind about that. I have something to tell you.

She looks questioningly from KAATRI *to* ERIK, *who nod
permission for her to speak.*

KAARLO.

Waiting, sits.

Yes? . . . Well?

MIRANDA.

Erik and Kaatri are going to be married.

KAARLO.

Erik?

He looks at him, wonderingly, and then bursts out laughing.

MIRANDA.

Reproachfully.

Kaarlo!

KAARLO.

Still laughing.

Forgive me—but——

MIRANDA.

Don't laugh. Now, it's not funny, Kaarlo.

KAARLO.

No. No.

MIRANDA.

No.

KAARLO.

No, I know it isn't.

MIRANDA.

Darling—you should congratulate them at least.

ERIK.

Oh, let him laugh, Mother. Perhaps it *is* funny.

KAARLO.

No, no.

Rises.

I *do* congratulate you, Erik. And as for you, Kaatri—

She rises as he goes to her.

—you're a sweet girl and I shall be delighted to have you for a daughter-in-law.

He kisses her.

KAATRI.

Curtsying.

Thank you, Dr. Valkonen.

KAARLO.

Ever since Erik was born I've been training him to be a gentleman of taste and discrimination, and, by God, I've succeeded.

To ERIK.

Again I congratulate you and thank you for justifying me. It's really—it's unbelievable. *You*—a bridegroom!

He kisses him.

But we must have some schnapps—a toast to the happy couple. And then we will all have supper.

MIRANDA.

Oh darling, we're having supper later, tonight. I told the maids they could go to church. And we're all going to church, too. Come with us, Kaarlo. You must go and put on your tail coat.

KAARLO.

And why must we all go to church?

MIRANDA.

Oh, there's going to be a great service. The President and everybody will be there. We're going to pray that this country will be able to defend itself.

KAARLO'S *amusement fades instantly.*

KAARLO.

Oh! So that's it! All day I have had the utmost difficulty persuading my assistants to attend to their duties. All they wanted to think about and talk about was would we or would we not have to fight the Soviet Union? I don't want to hear any of that talk here.

MIRANDA.

Neither do I, Kaarlo. But I've had to hear it. Erik is ready to fight.

KAARLO.

Erik?

He turns coldly to ERIK.

You're a child. It seems to me that you are deciding too suddenly that you are grown up. If you want to consider yourself engaged to be married, I have no objection— I'm delighted. But I don't want to hear that you are talking to your mother, or to any one else, about going to war.

ERIK.

I'm sorry, Father—but I have to do what I think best.

KAARLO.

And are you *able* to think?

MIRANDA.

Oh, Kaarlo! Of course Erik knows——

KAARLO.

No, Miranda. Don't interrupt.

To ERIK.

I repeat—in forming this heroic resolve to fight—have you used one grain of the intelligence that I know you possess?

206

ERIK.

I hope I have.

KAARLO.

Hoping is not good enough. You have seen those celebrations in Red Square—all those aeroplanes, those huge tanks, those troops marching—hundreds of thousands of them?

ERIK.

Yes, Father—I've seen them.

KAARLO.

And yet you dare to pretend you're competent to stand up against such a force as that?

ERIK.

That's why I've trained with the volunteer ski troops—and why I've worked to help make the Mannerheim Line so strong they can never break through.

KAARLO.

All that nonsensical child's play on skis——

ERIK.

Kaatri's brother Vaino is younger than I am—but he's with his father's regiment at the frontier . . .

KAARLO.

   Bitterly.

Oh! If we are at war with the Soviet Union, *I* shall be at the frontier, too. Surely we'll need everybody, including the aged and decrepit.

MIRANDA.

Now, really, Kaarlo, that is just simply ridiculous——

KAARLO.

Sitting.

I can press the trigger of a machine gun just as well as Erik. . . . So that's what we're going to pray for? Ability to imitate our enemies in the display of force. It is all nothing but a substitute for intelligent thinking.

ERIK.

This is not a time for intelligent thinking! That doesn't do any good.

KAARLO.

No?

ERIK.

When your enemies are relying on force, you can't meet them with theories. You can't throw books at them—even good books. What else can anybody do but fight?

KAARLO.

Bitterly.

This is no time for intelligent thinking! So this is the climax of a century of scientific miracles. This is what the great men worked for—what *they* fought for in their laboratories. Pasteur, Koch, Ehrlich, Lister. They saved lives that we might build Mannerheim Lines in which to die.

Church bells are heard faintly in the distance.

MIRANDA.

Now—that's enough, Kaarlo.

Rising.

If you don't want to go to church, you don't have to. We'll go by ourselves.

KAARLO.

Rising.

Oh, I'll put on my tail coat and go with you. I'll join in asking God to grant the impossible. But I reserve the right to say my own prayers.

He goes out. MIRANDA, *who has been putting on her hat and coat, crosses to* ERIK.

MIRANDA.

We'll be ready in a few minutes. And, Erik—you must not say any more to your father about going to war.

ERIK.

I'll try not to, Mother.

MIRANDA *goes out.*

Poor father! This is a terrible thing for him—for a man of great faith, as he is. The rest of us have nothing to lose but our lives.

KAATRI *goes to* ERIK—*takes hold of him.*

KAATRI.

Erik—I love you—I do love you, and I'm sorry I said things tonight that only made you more unhappy. I wasn't much help to you.

ERIK.

Holding her tightly.

All you said was true, Kaatri. I'm glad you said it. I have to see things clearly. I have to see my mother and father as they are. They don't really live in this country—in this time. They live together in the future—the future as my father has imagined it—not the one that may be made by unimaginative men. They are wonderful people—both of them—wonderful and unreal. You *are* real. You know

what we have to face—and we will face it without fear.
He kisses her, passionately.

KAARLO.
Entering.
This coat reeks of moth balls. It will be a scandal in church.

MIRANDA.
Offstage.
Don't worry, Kaarlo. There'll be so much of that smell in church they won't even notice you. Have you a clean handkerchief?

KAARLO.
Will you bring me one, please?
ERIK helps KAARLO with his coat.
Get your coat on, Kaatri, my dear—and you too, Erik.

ERIK.
Yes, Father.
ERIK and KAATRI go out. MIRANDA enters, and puts a handkerchief into KAARLO's coat pocket. He kisses her cheek.

KAARLO.
Come, Miranda—we go to pray.
They start out toward the right.
O God, have pity, for that which we have greatly feared has come upon us.
He switches off the lights. The room is in darkness, except for the moonlight from the windows. The church bells can still be heard.

CURTAIN

SCENE III

The same. Next afternoon.

UNCLE WALDEMAR *comes in from the right, and is surprised to see black drapes at all the windows. They are now drawn apart to let the sun in. He inspects them, goes to the piano, sits, starts to play.*

MIRANDA *calls from the dining room.*

MIRANDA'S VOICE.
Uncle Waldemar!

UNCLE WALDEMAR.
Yes?

MIRANDA'S VOICE.
Are Kaarlo and Erik with you?

UNCLE WALDEMAR.
No.

MIRANDA *comes in from the dining room. She is wearing
an apron and carrying a dust cloth.*

MIRANDA.
Have you seen them?

UNCLE WALDEMAR.
I saw Kaarlo. I stopped at the hospital.

MIRANDA.
Is he all right?

UNCLE WALDEMAR.
Yes.
Greatly relieved, she kisses him.

MIRANDA.
And Erik?

UNCLE WALDEMAR.
Oh, I don't know anything about him. I thought he was
here.

MIRANDA.
I haven't seen him since the church service last night. He
took Kaatri home and got in very late and then he was
off this morning even before I was up.

UNCLE WALDEMAR.
Probably he's with Kaatri now, at the Alquists' house.

MIRANDA.
Did any bombs fall in that part of the city?

UNCLE WALDEMAR.
No. I passed there on my way home. There was no damage there.

MIRANDA.

Was the air raid bad?

UNCLE WALDEMAR.

Not nearly as bad as expected. Maybe about thirty people killed.

MIRANDA.

That's what the policeman told me.

UNCLE WALDEMAR.

Were the police here?

MIRANDA.

Yes, I was ordered to put up those black curtains on the windows before nightfall. There must be no light from the windows. . . . Oh, I'm so glad to see you, Uncle Waldemar. I've been alone here all day . . .

UNCLE WALDEMAR.

Alone? Where are Ilma and Lempi?

MIRANDA.

They're gone. They're both in the Lottas. From now on all of us will have to eat my cooking. It's three o'clock in the afternoon, and I just finished making the beds. They look frightful. . . . I wish Kaarlo and Erik would come home! What was Kaarlo doing at the hospital?

UNCLE WALDEMAR.

I don't know. I saw him only for a moment. He had a white coat on.

MIRANDA *starts dusting the furniture.*

MIRANDA.

When he left here this morning for the hospital, he said it was a good joke—his trying to be a doctor again—when it's been fifteen years since he even gave anybody an aspirin tablet.

UNCLE WALDEMAR.

Coming down from the piano.
Miranda——

MIRANDA.

Yes, Uncle Waldemar.
She is kneeling, dusting.

UNCLE WALDEMAR.

With apparent difficulty.
Miranda, I want to tell you that I am sorry for many things that I have said.

MIRANDA.

What things?

UNCLE WALDEMAR.

I've talked too much about the troubles of the world.

MIRANDA.

And why should you feel you have to apologize for that?

UNCLE WALDEMAR.

Because now I am deeply distressed.

MIRANDA.

I know you are. We're all distressed. But there's nothing we can do about it.

UNCLE WALDEMAR.

I have been a poor companion for you and Kaarlo. It wasn't so bad for Kaarlo because he paid no attention. But you have been so good and kind—to me and all of us here. You came here a stranger, and you made all of us love you.

MIRANDA.

Harshly.

Now, for God's sake, Uncle Waldemar, don't let's have any of that!

UNCLE WALDEMAR.

But there are things on my mind, and I want to say them. You have worked so hard and so well to make this a happy home——

MIRANDA.

Dusting the sofa.

I've never done any work in my life, and I've never wanted to.

UNCLE WALDEMAR.

But you have filled this house with laughter—your own peculiar American kind of laughter. And here I have been, in the midst of all this happiness, an apostle of despair.

MIRANDA.

And so you want to be forgiven for telling the truth?

UNCLE WALDEMAR.

With bitter self-accusation.

I should have had more philosophy! I—who lived for forty years under the tyranny of the Tsars—and then saw my country rise up from the ashes of the war and the revolution. I should have been reconciled to this. And you—you never saw anything of such real misery in your country. But now—when this came—you took it calmly. You showed wisdom.

MIRANDA.

I took it calmly because I didn't know what was coming.

I never believed it could happen. I don't believe it now. Look at me, dusting the furniture in the face of the enemy! Did you ever see such a confession of utter helplessness?

She tosses the dust rag aside and sits down on the sofa.

UNCLE WALDEMAR.

You like to believe you are merely frivolous. But you're not so foreign to us solemn Finns as you think. You're a daughter of the Puritans, who would resist any oppression, undergo any sacrifice, in order to worship God in their own way. . . . I have always believed in God's mercy. I have served Him in His church. Whenever I was in doubt and fear, I would go back to the teachings of Martin Luther—to the doctrine of "The Freedom of the Christian Man." And then I would believe again that the virtues of simple faith would always triumph over intolerance. Whenever I had enough money saved, I would go to Germany, to Eisenach, to the room in the Wartburg where Luther worked. "A mighty fortress is our God." But last year when I was there I saw the Nazis. I saw old friends of mine, living in terror—some of them because they have Jewish blood—some just because they retain a sense of common decency. Even ministers of the gospel —afraid that if they preached the true devotion to God's word they would go into concentration camps. I saw men marching—marching—marching.

MIRANDA *rises and begins to dust again.*

Day and night, singing "Today we own Germany—tomorrow the whole world." They didn't know where they were marching to. They didn't care. They had been drilled and lectured down to the level where marching itself was enough. I was with one of my friends, an old musician like me, and we were looking from the windows of his house. Across the street a truckload of young Nazis had pulled up and they were wrecking the home of a Jewish dentist. They wanted to take the gold he used to put in people's teeth. They were doing it systematically, as the Germans do everything. And my friend whispered to me—for he did not dare raise his voice, even in his own home—he said, "They say they are doing this to fight Bolshevism. It is a lie! For they *are* Bolshevism!" And that is the truth. . . . "Today we own Germany, tomorrow the whole world." Including Russia.

MIRANDA.
Coming close to him.
They can't win, Uncle Waldemar.

UNCLE WALDEMAR.
Rises and looks out the window.
Can *we* prevent them from winning? All we can do is defend ourselves to the end. And then they sweep over us to the next goal—and the next——

MIRANDA.
You're a good Christian, Uncle Waldemar. You have to believe that they can't win.

UNCLE WALDEMAR.
Passionately.
I can believe in the coming of the anti-Christ. I can believe in the Apocalypse. "And Satan shall be loosed out of his prison, and shall go out to deceive the nations which are in the four quarters of the earth."
MIRANDA *dusts the keys of the piano.* ERIK *comes in at the right. He is wearing the uniform of the ski troops.*

ERIK.

Mother—I have to leave in a few minutes—

He sees her face as she looks at him. There is a long pause. ERIK *takes off his hat. Finally she crosses to him.* Mother, I'm going into the north with a detachment of ski troops. I don't know just where we're being sent, but we're to assemble at the station in an hour.

MIRANDA.

Is Kaatri going with you?

ERIK.

No. She'll be at the station, but she doesn't know yet what they want her to do. I have to fix up my pack right away.

MIRANDA.

You'll want some food for the journey. I'll get some for you. . . .

He kisses her cheek.

Whatever we have in the kitchen——

ERIK.

Thank you, Mother.

He goes out at the right.

MIRANDA.

To UNCLE WALDEMAR.

If I'd only known about this sooner, I'd have gotten some things in. I—I suppose there's some canned stuff. . . . (*She seems helpless, despairing.*)

UNCLE WALDEMAR.

Rising.

I'll help you look, Miranda.

As they both go toward the dining room.

I'm sure there are plenty of good things we can find for Erik.

KAARLO'S VOICE.
From off, right.
Miranda!
> MIRANDA *stops short.* UNCLE WALDEMAR *goes on out, into the kitchen.*

MIRANDA.
Kaarlo?

KAARLO.
Entering.
Yes. Miranda—look who has come back to Helsinki! Mr. Corween, you remember him?
> DAVE *comes in and goes to* MIRANDA.

MIRANDA.
Of course.

DAVE.
I'm so glad to see you again, Mrs. Valkonen.

KAARLO.
I just met him. He arrived only this morning, and he was on his way to see us.
> *He goes to her and kisses her.*
It was awful, not being able to telephone?—But you're all right?

MIRANDA.
Yes.

KAARLO.
And Erik?

MIRANDA.
Yes. He's here. He——

KAARLO.

But—sit down, Mr. Corween. What will you have to drink?

MIRANDA.

Kaarlo——

KAARLO.

To DAVE.

Excuse me. Yes, my dear——

MIRANDA.

Kaarlo! Erik is going into the army. He's upstairs, now, packing his things.

KAARLO.

Where is he going?

MIRANDA.

I don't know. Into the north somewhere.

MIRANDA *goes to* DAVE.

Do you think there will be much fighting in the north, Mr. Corween?

DAVE.

You know more about the situation than I do, Mrs. Valkonen.

MIRANDA.·

You'll forgive me, Mr. Corween. I have something to do.

DAVE.

Of course.

MIRANDA *goes out into the kitchen.*

I think you'd like me to go, Dr. Valkonen.

KAARLO.

No, no. Sit down, sit down. Are you going to stay here for a while in Helsinki—or is this another flying visit?

DAVE.

Sitting.

I don't know how long I shall stay. It—it all depends.

KAARLO.

You'll be broadcasting from here?

DAVE.

Oh, yes, Doctor. The American public likes to be kept in touch with all that's going on.

KAARLO.

That's good. We like to keep in touch with them.
He is making a gallant attempt to sustain polite conversation.
We heard your broadcasts from Warsaw. They were brilliant.

DAVE.

Thank you. I can't say I enjoyed them very much.

KAARLO.

Sitting—quietly.

It was tragic, wasn't it!

DAVE.

Yes, it was. Dr Valkonen, I know that this is no time for me to be bothering you or your wife, but——

KAARLO.

You are more than welcome here, my dear friend.

DAVE.

I know that, Doctor. But there's something I want to say.

KAARLO.

Yes?

DAVE.

I saw Jim Walsh at the American Legation.

KAARLO.

Yes—yes.

DAVE.

He is very fond of you and Mrs. Valkonen.

KAARLO.

Thank you.

DAVE.

As he should be. He asked me to beg you to leave Finland at once.

KAARLO *looks at him.*

He can arrange everything. A ship has been chartered next Tuesday from Goteborg, for New York. It is to take hundreds of American refugees. Mr. Walsh can arrange passage for you and Mrs. Valkonen. He can get you to Sweden by plane. But—he must know about it at once.

KAARLO.

Well, now—that's very kind of Mr. Walsh, especially when he's so busy.

DAVE.

Earnestly.

I hope you will do it, Dr. Valkonen.

KAARLO.

You mean—go?

DAVE.

Yes—and at once.

KAARLO.

I am needed here for the time being. There is a great shortage of doctors. All of the young men in all the hospitals are going to the front, for service with the army medical corps. There will be many more casualties here from air raids.

DAVE.

It's not my business to say so, Doctor—but that isn't suitable work for a winner of the Nobel Prize.

KAARLO.

With great sadness.
It is not suitable work for any member of the human race, Mr. Corween. But someone must do it.

DAVE.

I realize that you're a patriotic citizen of this country——

KAARLO.

I am not a patriotic citizen of this country, Mr. Corween. I hope I am aware of the fact that "patriotism" as now practiced is one of the most virulent manifestations of evil.

DAVE.

Yes, Doctor. That's just what I mean. You're a citizen of the world. You're of importance to the whole world, not just to these few gallant men who are going to fight and die for Finland. . . . Oh—I know it's presumptuous of me to be talking to you. But—I beg you, please, for God's sake, while you still have the chance, go to a country where you can carry on your work—your own fight —to bring men to consciousness——

KAARLO.

But I shall carry on that work as long as I live, Mr. Corween—wherever I am.

DAVE.

As long as you live! I'm sorry if I seem unduly emotional about it, Doctor—but—I have seen too many men of intellectual distinction forced into uniform, forced to pick up guns and shoot because they had discovered that their intelligence was impotent to cope with brutal reality. *You* may be forced into that situation, Dr. Valkonen. You who have devoted yourself to discovering the inward defenses of man. You may find yourself crouching behind a sandbag, shooting at an illiterate Russian peasant.

KAARLO.

Yes, Mr. Corween. You know whereof you speak. And I should be the last to dispute you. Now—we feel like heroes, strong in the armor of the justice of our own cause. Soon—we may be corpses. It is all very foolish—very temporary. But, you see, I am accustomed to this sort of thing. In my youth, this country was ruled by the Romanovs. I survived that oppression. I am prepared to endure it again. Let the forces of evil engulf us. If the truth is in here, my friend——

He taps his heart. MIRANDA *comes in with* ERIK.

MIRANDA.

Kaarlo, Erik must go now.

DAVE.

He knows he must get out before the possibly painful farewells are said.

I'm afraid I must go now. (*To* ERIK.) How do you do?

I—I have to get back to the hotel, to stand by for orders from New York. I'll be at the Kamp, Mrs. Valkonen, and I hope I'll see you soon again. Good-bye, Doctor. Good-bye, Mrs. Valkonen.

ERIK.

Good-bye.

MIRANDA.

You must come to see us often.

DAVE.

Thank you, I shall. Good-bye. Good luck.

DAVE *goes out. There is a moment of tense silence. No one knows quite what to say.*

KAARLO.

To ERIK.

You're leaving now?

ERIK.

Yes, Father. We're to be at the station at five o'clock. I—I'd better go at once. I don't want to be late.

To MIRANDA.

Where's Uncle Waldemar?

MIRANDA.

He's bringing the food for you from the kitchen. You'll be able to say good-bye to him on the way out.

KAARLO.

I take it you know what you're doing—what chances you have of accomplishing anything.

ERIK.

Yes, Father. I think I know about that.

KAARLO.

Very well, then. There's nothing I can say to you but good-bye.

ERIK.

To KAARLO.

Father, before I go, I want you to know that I'm sorry for you. I think I understand what this is for you. It's worse for you than it is for any of us. But—if it's any consolation to you—I hope you'll remember—you have a son who at least obeys the Fourth Commandment. I honor my father and my mother.

> *The emotion of this is a bit too much for* ERIK. *He hides his face in his hands.* KAARLO *leans over and kisses him tenderly.*

KAARLO.

Go on, go on, Erik.

> ERIK *turns from him toward* MIRANDA.

MIRANDA.

I'll go to the door with you, darling.

> *They go out.* KAARLO *is alone. He goes to a chair at the extreme left, sits down, looks out the window, lost, helpless.* MIRANDA *returns and sits on the couch at the right.*

KAARLO.

Almost angrily.

I suppose you want to weep now? Then you'd better go to our room and get it over with.

MIRANDA.

What good will it do to weep? I've never in my life understood what it is to enjoy the luxury of a good cry.

She rises suddenly.
I'm going to the kitchen.

KAARLO.
What for?

MIRANDA.
I don't know. I have to start trying to learn how to cook.
She goes out. KAARLO *looks after her miserably. After a moment,* UNCLE WALDEMAR *comes in.*

UNCLE WALDEMAR.
Kaarlo. . . . Kaarlo——

KAARLO.
Yes.

UNCLE WALDEMAR.
Dr. Ziemssen is here.

KAARLO.
Dr. Ziemssen?

UNCLE WALDEMAR.
He has come to say good-bye. He is going back to Germany.

KAARLO.
Oh. . . . Very well, I'll see him.

UNCLE WALDEMAR.
Going off at the right.
Come in, Dr. Ziemssen.
DR. ZIEMSSEN *comes in. He is wearing his overcoat, carrying his hat and walking stick.* UNCLE WALDEMAR *closes the door behind him.*

KAARLO.
I'm delighted you came in. Let me take your coat.

ZIEMSSEN.

Thank you, no, Herr Doktor. I can stay but a short time.

KAARLO.

Please sit down.

ZIEMSSEN.

I know this is not an opportune moment. I saw Erik go. I saluted him—a splendid young soldier. You have good cause to be proud.

KAARLO.

As they sit on the sofa.

Thank you, Dr. Ziemssen. I'm sorry to hear you're going. I've greatly enjoyed our discussions at the Institute. But —I can well understand that this is not the place for you under the circumstances.

ZIEMSSEN.

Seriously.

It is not the place for you, either, Dr. Valkonen. I advise you also to go.

KAARLO.

Go?

ZIEMSSEN.

Leave Finland. Leave Europe at once!

KAARLO.

Why is everybody ordering me out of my home? Mr. Corween was here also telling me I must leave.

ZIEMSSEN.

Mr. Corween is a remarkably well-informed man. He is aware of the inevitable outcome of this war, as you yourself must be, Herr Doktor. Oh—I have all admiration for the little Finnish army. But two hundred thousand against ten million——

KAARLO.

Yes, we will be conquered, as we have been conquered before. And then we will be ruled from Moscow—as we were formerly ruled from Petersburg. But as I was just saying to Mr. Corween, I shall continue with my experiments.

ZIEMSSEN.

Dr. Valkonen—I must warn you—you are making a serious mistake!

KAARLO.

Mistake?

ZIEMSSEN.

You are judging this situation in terms of the past.

KAARLO.

One can only judge by one's own experience.

ZIEMSSEN.

Precisely. Your own experience is misleading.

KAARLO.

In what way, Dr. Ziemssen?

ZIEMSSEN.

That is just what I wish to tell you. You think our enemies are these—these Communists who now invade your country?

KAARLO.

Yes. That is what I think.

ZIEMSSEN.

The Russians think so, too, but they are wrong. *We* are your enemies, Herr Doktor. This Finnish incident is one little item in our vast scheme. We make good use of our esteemed allies of the Soviet Union. All the little communist cells, in labor movements, youth movements, in all nations—they are now working for *us*, although they may not know it. Communism is a good laxative to loosen the constricted bowels of democracy. When it has served that purpose, it will disappear down the sewer with the excrement that must be purged.

KAARLO.

It seems to me, Dr. Ziemssen, you are talking with extremely undiplomatic frankness.

ZIEMSSEN.

I know I can do so to you, Herr Doktor. You are a scientist. You are accustomed to face facts—even those facts which to the ordinary, dull mind are too terrible to contemplate.

KAARLO.

What is it you are threatening, Doctor? What is going to happen to Finland?

ZIEMSSEN.

You do not know the whole story of what happened to Poland!

KAARLO *looks at him, rises, and walks away.*

You will hear the Pope in Rome weeping publicly and proclaiming that the Polish nation will rise again. I assure you it will not rise again, because, as a nation, it is dead. The same is true of every nation that we conquer;

we shall see to it that none of them will ever rise again. Today, the remnants of the Polish people are scattered all the way from the Rhine to the Pacific coast of Siberia. This is a process of annihilation. It is a studied technique, and it was not invented in Moscow. You will find the blueprints of it, not in *Das Kapital,* but in *Mein Kampf.* It is all there for you to read. It involves, first, liquidation of all leaders of thought—political, religious, economic, intellectual.

KAARLO *sits down. He seems to slump.*

Among the masses—the difficult ones are killed—the weaklings are allowed to die of starvation—the strong ones are enslaved.

KAARLO.

You are an anthropologist—a man of learning, Dr. Ziemssen. Do you approve of this technique?

ZIEMSSEN.

Naturally, I regret the necessity for it. But I *admit* the necessity. And so must you, Dr. Valkonen. Remember that every great state of the past in its stages of construction has required slavery. Today, the greatest world state is in process of formation. There is a great need for slave labor. And—these Finns and Scandinavians would be useful. They are strong; they have great capacity for endurance. Is that brutal—ruthless? Yes. But I am now talking to a scientist, not a sniveling sentimentalist. Vivisection has been called brutal, ruthless—but it is necessary for the survival of man. So it is necessary that inferior races be considered merely as animals. . . . Do you believe me, Herr Doktor?

KAARLO.

I believe you. Although—still talking as one scientist to another—I cannot help wondering just how you establish proof that these other races are inferior, especially when you know it is a lie.

ZIEMSSEN.

Of course it is a lie, biologically. But we can prove it by the very simple expedient of asserting our own superiority—just as the Romans did before they decayed—and the Anglo-Saxons, before *they* decayed. View this objectively, Herr Doktor, and then you will be able to proceed with your experiments. You have made important progress in an important field—conditioning men to their environment. That can be of extraordinary value to us in the future. You can help to postpone, perhaps indefinitely, the time when *we* will be conquered by decay. But, first—you must accept the theory of the new world state, for that *is* the environment of the future. If you refuse to accept, and stay here and attempt to resist destiny, you will die.

KAARLO.

Where can one go to escape this world state?

ZIEMSSEN.

Smiles.

An intelligent question, Herr Doktor. I assure you that the United States is secure for the present. It may continue so for a long time, if the Americans refrain from interfering with us in Mexico and South America and Canada. And I believe they will refrain. They are now showing far greater intelligence in that respect than ever

232

before. They are learning to mind their own shrinking business.

KAARLO.

I appreciate your motives in warning me, Dr. Ziemssen. And I understand that all you have told me is confidential.

ZIEMSSEN.
Laughing.
You *are* an innocent, my friend! Nothing that I have said is confidential. You may repeat it all. And you will not be believed. There is the proof of our superiority—that our objectives are so vast that our pigmy-minded enemies simply have not the capacity to believe them. They are eager to accept the big lies we give them, because they cannot comprehend the big truth.
Rises.
And the big truth is this: For the first time since the whole surface of the earth became known, one dynamic race is on the march to occupy that surface and rule it! When you have absorbed that huge conception, you will find that your own theories can be adjusted to it. And now I must go.
He extends his hand to KAARLO.
But I advise you to make haste, Herr Doktor. Finland's only lines of communication are through Sweden and Norway. We have many means of cutting those lines. Goodbye, Herr Doktor. I said good-bye. I hope we part friends.
He goes to the door.
KAARLO *nods as he shakes hands with* DR. ZIEMSSEN.
My compliments to Frau Valkonen. Good-bye.
He goes.

UNCLE WALDEMAR'S VOICE.
Heard offstage.
Good-bye, Dr. Ziemssen.

ZIEMSSEN'S VOICE.
Good-bye, Herr Sederstrum. I have enjoyed your music.
KAARLO *crosses and stands behind the sofa.* UNCLE
WALDEMAR *enters, switches on lights, goes immediately
to the windows and starts closing the black curtains.*
KAARLO *looks toward the kitchen.*

KAARLO.
Uncle Waldemar—Uncle Waldemar——

UNCLE WALDEMAR.
Yes. . . . What is it?
Having fixed the windows, UNCLE WALDEMAR *turns to*
KAARLO.

KAARLO.
Get your hat and coat on.

UNCLE WALDEMAR.
What for?

KAARLO.
I want you to go to the American Legation and see Mr.
Walsh. Tell him that Mrs. Valkonen will leave on that
ship Mr. Corween told me about. I believe it sails from
Goteborg on Tuesday. He must make all the necessary
arrangements at once. Find out what is the earliest possible moment she can leave for Sweden. Ask him if it is
safe by aeroplane.

UNCLE WALDEMAR.
You're sending Miranda away—alone?

KAARLO.

Yes. Be quiet. She's right there in the kitchen.

UNCLE WALDEMAR.

You think you can persuade her to do this?

KAARLO.

I have to persuade her, and if necessary, you will help me. You know what has happened to Poland.

UNCLE WALDEMAR.

Yes, I know. But Miranda doesn't care about those things. She doesn't believe them.

KAARLO.

I didn't believe them either. . . . But—I'll find another way of persuading her. If ruthlessness is the order of this day, then I shall be ruthless, too. I will tell her I don't want her here. She is of no use in a time like this.

UNCLE WALDEMAR.

That will hurt her more deeply than the Russians ever could.

KAARLO.

She will recover from that hurt. Go ahead!

UNCLE WALDEMAR.

Very well.

He starts to go, but MIRANDA *enters. She is carrying a tray on which are a coffee pot and cups.*

MIRANDA.

Uncle Waldemar—I made some coffee. Would you like some?

UNCLE WALDEMAR.

No, thank you.

MIRANDA.

I tasted it. It's quite good.

UNCLE WALDEMAR.

Thank you—but I have to go.

MIRANDA.

Where?

UNCLE WALDEMAR.

I want to have some exercise and fresh air.

MIRANDA.

But you've been out all day.

UNCLE WALDEMAR.

Even so—I'm going out again.
He goes out. MIRANDA *takes the tray over to the piano
and puts it down.*

MIRANDA.

Poor Uncle Waldemar—all this has upset him terribly....
Will you have some coffee, Kaarlo?

KAARLO.

No, thank you.

MIRANDA.

I wish you'd try it.

KAARLO.

Later, perhaps. . . . Please sit down.

MIRANDA.

What is it, Kaarlo? Did you want to talk about Erik?
She starts to go out.

KAARLO.

No—I do not want to talk about Erik. Please sit down.

She sits down and looks at him, curiously.
I wish to tell you, my dear, that the time has come for you to go home.

MIRANDA.
Home? This is my home.

KAARLO.
I mean—to your own country. To America.

MIRANDA.
Amazed.
Why?

KAARLO.
Because I do not wish you to stay here. Mr. Walsh at the American Legation can make all the necessary arrangements. You will probably leave for Sweden tomorrow—perhaps even tonight. We will hear soon about that. You can then go to Boston and stay with your aunt.

MIRANDA.
Will you go with me?

KAARLO.
Naturally not. I am needed here. You will stay in America until this business is over.

MIRANDA.
And when it *is* over? What then?

KAARLO.
Why—you'll come back here, and we'll go right on living as we've always done. I might come to America and fetch you.

MIRANDA.
Supposing you were killed?

KAARLO.

I—killed? I'm a doctor.

MIRANDA.

And do you suppose a Russian in a bombing plane ten thousand feet up can tell the difference between an ordinary person and a winner of the Nobel Prize?

KAARLO.

It is out of the question that I should go. Freud left Vienna after the Nazi occupation. He went to London, and he was welcomed there, he was honored. But—he couldn't speak. He knew that if he told the truth, it would be printed, and his own people, still in Austria, would be made to suffer for it, horribly. . . . So Freud was technically free—but he was silenced. What did he then have to live for? Nothing. . . . So he died. . . . No—I will not leave. You must go alone.

MIRANDA.

And if I left here—what would *I* have to live for?

KAARLO.

Oh, you'll manage very well in your own great, secure, distant country.

He has been moving about the room. Her eyes have been following him, questioning him, seeking him out, with every word, every move.

MIRANDA.

Kaarlo! Tell me the truth. Why do you want me to go?

KAARLO.

What can you do here? This is a war for the defense of Finland. It must be fought by the Finnish people.

She is staring at him. He is avoiding her gaze.
This country becomes an armed camp. Every one of us knows what he must do, or she must do, and is trained to do it. Are you trained for anything, but wearing lovely clothes, being a charming hostess?
She looks at him, helplessly.
You are an intelligent woman, Miranda. Reason this out for yourself. You will see that this is a time when everyone who eats bread must have worked to earn it. And, God help us, there is only one form of work that matters now—resistance—blind, dogged, desperate resistance.

MIRANDA.
Rising, and following him.
You've said yourself—that kind of resistance is useless.
She is trying desperately to score a point. He is trying desperately to avoid being scored on, though ever conscious of his vulnerability.

KAARLO.
Angrily.
You don't know what I've said. Or—if you know the words, you have less idea of their meaning than the youngest of the students who hear my lectures at the Institute. I'm not insulting your courage, Miranda. Nor your good will. I'm sure you would like to be useful. But you can't. You know you can't.

MIRANDA.
You think it would be impossible for me to contribute anything—to help in any way?

KAARLO.
Why do I have to tell you what you must know yourself?

239

MIRANDA *looks at him with a look almost of bitter hostility. She turns and walks away. Unutterably miserable, he looks after her. The artifice of his frigid superiority is beginning to crumple.*

There is no reason for you to be ashamed of this. This is not your country. It is not your war.

MIRANDA.

This is the country of my husband and my son.

KAARLO.

And do you think Erik and I want you to be caught in these ruins?

MIRANDA.

You have no right to speak of Erik! I don't think he would be particularly happy or proud to hear that his mother has scurried to safety at the first sound of a shot fired.

KAARLO.

Erik has American blood in his viens. He will understand.

MIRANDA.

Flaming.

Oh! So that's it! His American blood will tell him that it's perfectly reasonable for me to run away. You evidently share Kaatri's opinion of me.

KAARLO.

Desperately.

Don't put words into my mouth that I have not uttered——

MIRANDA.

Turning on him, suddenly coming to him.

240

Then don't be afraid to come out and say what you mean. It's obvious that you don't want me here, because I'm incompetent—I'm a parasite—I'm a non-essential. In all these years that we've been together nothing has happened to disturb the lovely serenity of our home. And now comes this great calamity. And immediately you decide that you don't want me—you don't need me.

KAARLO.

I didn't say that!

MIRANDA.

Then what did you say?

KAARLO is obviously making a last effort to control himself.

KAARLO.

Miranda! You don't understand why I want you to go!

MIRANDA.

It makes no difference to me whether I understand it or not. There's one thing I do know, and you'd better know it, too: I am not going. Probably, you *don't* need me. You have important work to do—and I'm sure that's enough, for you. But the time may come when Erik might need me, and when that time comes, I intend to be here——

KAARLO.

No, please—for God's sake—don't keep on bringing Erik into it! Wasn't it bad enough to see him going away like that, in his uniform? That poor, hopeful, defenseless child!

He sees that he has hurt her, terribly, with that.

Oh—I'm sorry, darling. You must see that I've been making a desperate attempt to drive you to safety with lies.

It's no use. You always can make me tell the truth. The real trouble is—you've had too much confidence in me. How could you know that I was living in a dream—a beautiful, wishful dream in which you played your own unsubstantial but exciting part? And now—there is war —and our own son goes to fight—and I wake up to discover that reality itself is a hideous nightmare. . . . I shouldn't be talking to you like this, Miranda. I'm frightened.

MIRANDA.

You can never be afraid to say anything to me, darling.

KAARLO.

I have suddenly realized what and where I am. I am a man working in the apparent security of a laboratory. I am working on a theory so tentative that it may take hundreds of years of research, and generations of workers, to prove it. I am trying to defeat insanity—degeneration of the human race. . . . And then—a band of pyromaniacs enters the building in which I work. And that building is the world—the whole planet—not just Finland. They set fire to it. What can I do? Until that fire is put out, there can be no peace—no freedom from fear —no hope of progress for mankind. . . . Every day that we hold them off—will only serve to increase the terror of the vengeance which must surely descend upon us. All the pathetic survivors of this war will have to pay in torture for the heroism of the dead. And it isn't just us— not just this one little breed that wants to be free. This is a war for everybody—yes—even for the scientists who thought themselves immune behind their test tubes.
He looks into her eyes again.

Darling! I can stand this ordeal if I know it is only for myself. I can stand it if I know you are safe—that you are beyond their reach. . . . I love you. That is the only reality left to me. I love you.

They are in each other's arms. For a moment, they are silent.

MIRANDA.

Then I can stand it, too, darling, whatever it is. I can stand it as long as I know that you love me—that you do need me—that I am essential, after all. Even if I am a woman who is nothing but a woman. Even at a time when the whole life of the world is marching with men. . . .

They hold each other, closely. After a moment, she rises.

Now come and have some coffee.

They cross to the piano. She feels the coffee pot.

It's not very warm.

KAARLO.

It's no matter, darling. I'm sure it's good.

She is pouring the coffee.

CURTAIN

SCENE IV

The same. New Year's Day, 1940. Noon. There is a Christmas tree. There are many decorations on the tree, including a wide, white ribbon on which is an inscription in Finnish. At the top of the tree is a star.

UNCLE WALDEMAR *is at the piano playing something surprisingly spirited and gay.* KAARLO *comes in. He wears the uniform coat of a Colonel in the Medical Corps, but otherwise he is in civilian clothes. He is buttoning up the coat. As he glances back into the mirror, he looks rather sheepish and self-conscious.* UNCLE WALDEMAR *looks at him.*

KAARLO.

Well—Uncle Waldemar—haven't you anything to say about my new uniform?

UNCLE WALDEMAR.

What should I say? I've seen thousands of uniforms lately. They all look the same.

KAARLO.
Laughs.
I know. But—for some reason—when you see one on yourself, it seems to look better.

UNCLE WALDEMAR.
Stops playing, rises.
Are you trying to fool me, Kaarlo?

KAARLO.
Fool you? Why should I——?

UNCLE WALDEMAR.
You want me to think you are proud to be going?

KAARLO.
Gravely.
No, Uncle Waldemar.
He looks off to the kitchen, and then speaks confidentially.
When Erik went—I—I thought our world had come to an end. Since then—I have been struggling to adjust myself—to find in all this tragedy some intimation of hope for the future.

UNCLE WALDEMAR.
Tenderly.
I know, Kaarlo.

KAARLO.
This
Indicates his uniform coat.
represents the final stage in that attempt at adjustment. It is like the moment when a scientist knows he can no longer experiment with guinea pigs—he must now test his theories on human life itself. It is kill or cure.

245

UNCLE WALDEMAR.

What are those ribbons you are wearing?

KAARLO.

The order of St. Ann with Swords—the Cross of St. George's.

UNCLE WALDEMAR.

You're going into the Mannerheim Line wearing Russian decorations?

KAARLO.

Why not? I won them. Or—at any rate—they were given to me. You think I should leave them off?

MIRANDA comes in from the kitchen with a tray on which are a pitcher of eggnog and five punch glasses. She sees KAARLO'S *coat.*

MIRANDA.

What is that you are wearing?

KAARLO.

It is my uniform coat. I was just trying it on.

MIRANDA.

What for? What do you want with a uniform?

KAARLO.

Of course I should have one. I'm a Colonel in the Army Medical Corps.

MIRANDA.

Now don't tell me you want to look impressive. Why have you suddenly got a uniform?

KAARLO.

Because I have to, Miranda. I'm going to Viipuri.

MIRANDA.

Shocked.

When are you going?

KAARLO.

This afternoon, I believe. What is that on the tray you brought in?

MIRANDA.

It's eggnog. I promised Dave Corween I'd make some to celebrate New Year's. Why are they sending you to Viipuri?

KAARLO.

Nobody is sending me, Miranda. I'm going because I wish to. More hospital space has to be provided there, and I want to see that the work is done efficiently.

MIRANDA.

Why haven't you told me about this before? You knew about it, Uncle Waldemar?

UNCLE WALDEMAR.

He told me only today.

KAARLO.

Now really, Miranda. This is not to be taken so seriously. I am not going very far away, and I shall probably be back within a fortnight. In fact, Dave Corween is going with me and a Polish officer named Rutkowski. Dave is to broadcast from Viipuri. That proves there's no danger.

He starts to go out at the right.

MIRANDA.

How do you get to Viipuri?

247

KAARLO.

I go in style . . . in that new American ambulance that just arrived from France.

He goes out taking off his coat.

MIRANDA.

Looking after KAARLO.

He was afraid to tell me—wasn't he, Uncle Waldemar?

UNCLE WALDEMAR.

Kaarlo always likes to avoid unpleasant subjects . . . outside his laboratory.

MIRANDA.

Is there something serious happening?

UNCLE WALDEMAR.

Well—you know, Miranda—there is still war. They still attack.

MIRANDA.

But everything's going well for us, isn't it?

UNCLE WALDEMAR.

We're alive. That's more than any one expected.

MIRANDA.

Why do they want more hospitals at Viipuri? I thought there weren't many wounded.

UNCLE WALDEMAR.

That is because now most of the wounded are frozen to death before they can be brought in. When warmer weather comes—the fighting will be different. They will need hospitals—especially on the isthmus.

She considers this dreadful thought for a moment.

MIRANDA.

Desperately.

Oh, God—Uncle Waldemar. Why don't we hear from Erik? He has been gone a whole month—*why* don't we hear?

UNCLE WALDEMAR *comes to her.*

UNCLE WALDEMAR.

We know Erik is well. Kaarlo sees every casualty list—including even those who are sick. It's just that up there in the Arctic there is not much chance of sending letters.

The doorbell is heard.

MIRANDA.

There's the doorbell.

UNCLE WALDEMAR.

I'll go, Miranda.

UNCLE WALDEMAR *goes out.* VOICES *can be heard off at the right.*

How do you do, Mr. Corween?

DAVE.

Off.

How do you do, sir?

UNCLE WALDEMAR.

Off.

Happy New Year!

DAVE.

Off.

Happy New Year to you, sir!

UNCLE WALDEMAR.

Off.

Go right in.

DAVE.

Off.

Thank you.

DAVE *comes in. He is dressed for a cold journey.*

MIRANDA.

Dave! Happy New Year!

DAVE.

Happy New Year, Mrs. Valkonen.

MIRANDA.

Pointing to the tray.

I've kept my promise about the eggnog.

DAVE.

I'm afraid I'm going to overtax your hospitality. There are four other boys here, all going up with the ambulance.

MIRANDA.

Oh! Bring them all in.

DAVE.

Thank you.

He calls off.

Come in, boys. Come in, Major.

MAJOR RUTKOWSKI *comes in. He is a tired, tragic young Polish officer. He is followed almost at once by* JOE BURNETT, BEN GICHNER *and* FRANK OLMSTEAD. JOE *is tall, lean, wearing a smart, new aviator's uniform;* BEN *is stout and cheerful;* FRANK, *young, sensitive and serious-minded. Both* BEN *and* FRANK *wear uniforms of the American Ambulance Corps, with Red Cross insignia on the sleeves.*

250

DAVE.

Mrs. Valkonen—this is Major Rutkowski.

RUTKOWSKI.

Bows.

Madame.

MIRANDA.

How do you do?

DAVE.

And this is the American Expeditionary Force in Finland. Joe Burnett of Haverford, Pa.—

MIRANDA.

Shaking hands with each in turn.

How do you do?

DAVE.

Ben Gichner of Cincinnati.

MIRANDA.

I'm very glad to see you.

DAVE.

And Frank Olmstead of San Francisco. Mrs. Valkonen of New Bedford.

MIRANDA.

Happy New Year!

JOE.

Thank you, Mrs. Valkonen.

FRANK.

Thank you.

BEN.

And a very happy New Year to you, Madame.

MIRANDA.

I have some eggnog, gentlemen——

Their faces light up.

In the midst of war we still have some milk and eggs and rye whiskey and even a little cream. You start serving it, Dave—while I get some more glasses. Sit down, everybody.

She goes out through the dining room.

DAVE.

Crossing.

Come on, Joe.

JOE *and* FRANK *follow* DAVE *across.* BEN *and* RUTKOWSKI *are looking about the room.*

Now, boys, remember. No remarks about the horrors of war. I'm afraid Mrs. Valkonen feels pretty badly about her husband going.

JOE.

We'll be tactful, Dave.

RUTKOWSKI.

Quietly.

A lovely house. This would be the house of good people in any country.

BEN.

It's got a sort of nice, Victorian quality. I thought everything in Finland was moderne.

FRANK.

Who is looking at the photographs on the piano.

Look, Joe. . . . Dr. Jung, Alexis Carrel, President Masaryk——

DAVE.

Bringing drinks across to RUTKOWSKI *and* BEN.

Here you are, Major Rutkowski. Nourishing and stimulating—but apt to be dangerous.

> FRANK *is standing by the piano, playing a few bars of a swing tune.*

MIRANDA.

Offstage.

Have you tried it yet?

DAVE.

We were waiting for you, Mrs. Valkonen.

> MIRANDA *re-enters with a tray holding more glasses.* BEN *and* RUTKOWSKI *rise.* DAVE *takes the tray from her, goes to the serving table and pours drinks for* MIRANDA *and himself.*

MIRANDA.

Here you are—here are the glasses.

To FRANK.

Was that you playing?

FRANK.

Diffidently.

I wouldn't call it playing.

MIRANDA.

It is wonderful.

BEN.

Come on, Dave. I think you ought to make a little speech in behalf of all of us.

DAVE.

I'm not at my best without a mike and a coast-to-coast hook-up.

He raises his glass and addresses MIRANDA.
However, we want to tell you we're glad to be here, enjoying your gracious hospitality, and we hope that this New Year will bring you and yours health and happiness.

MIRANDA.
As the circle of men gathers about her.
Why, that was a charming speech, Dave. I wish the same to you, all of you, and I welcome you to this house and this country. And I'd like to sing the Polish national anthem and "The Star-Spangled Banner," but I don't know the words of either.

DAVE.
Laughs.
That's all right, Mrs. Valkonen. Neither do we.
They all drink.

JOE.
It's magnificent.

DAVE.
Mrs. Valkonen, it's better even than the Parker House Punch.

BEN.
Frankly, I love it.

FRANK.
So do I.

RUTKOWSKI.
I've never tasted anything quite like it before—but I'm glad to be introduced.

MIRANDA.
Thank you—thank you.

To FRANK.

Do go on playing. Help yourselves as long as it lasts. There are American cigarettes.

MIRANDA *sits on the sofa.* FRANK *goes to the piano and plays.*

DAVE.

Everybody admires your house, Mrs. Valkonen.

BEN.

Yes. I was just saying, it has a nice, old-fashioned quality.

RUTKOWSKI.

It is so graceful.

MIRANDA.

I'm glad you see it with the Christmas tree. That always makes it more cheerful.

FRANK.

Stops playing.

May I ask—what is the inscription on that ribbon?

MIRANDA.

It's Finnish for "Glory to God in the highest and, on earth, peace, good will to men."

A pause.

We have that on the tree every Christmas. It's a tradition in this country.

KAARLO.

Calling from off stage, at the right.

I'll be with you in a moment, gentlemen. I have to assemble my kit.

MIRANDA.

Calling to him.

Can I help you Kaarlo?

KAARLO.

Off.

No, thank you, my dear. Is the eggnog good, gentlemen?

DAVE.

It's superb!

BEN.

We're in no hurry to leave, Doctor. We're having a fine time.

MIRANDA.

Have all you gentlemen just arrived in Helsinki?

BEN.

We got here yesterday, ma'am. . . . I mean, Frank Olmstead and Joe Burnett and me. We came by ship from Paris to Norway. Major Rutkowski has been here since November.

MIRANDA.

Had you been in the war in Poland, Major?

RUTKOWSKI.

Yes, Madame, but it lasted only three weeks. I was in the cavalry.

MIRANDA.

How did you manage to get here?

RUTKOWSKI.

From Riga, Madame. The survivors of my regiment were driven over the Lithuanian border. I worked my way to Helsinki intending to go on through Sweden to France to join the Polish Legion there. But——

MIRANDA.

But—there was a war here, so you didn't have to look any further.

RUTKOWSKI.

Yes, Madame.

MIRANDA.

We used to listen to Dave when he was broadcasting from Warsaw, describing the incredible heroism during the siege. Day after day we'd hear the German official radio announcing that Warsaw had fallen and then, late at night, we'd hear the government's station, playing Chopin's "Polonaise," to let us know they were still there.

BEN.

We heard it, too, in Paris. It was thrilling.

DAVE.

What were you doing in Paris, Ben—if it isn't too personal a question?

BEN.

I was employed there! I worked for the American Express Company. I was a travel salesman.
   He turns to MIRANDA.
I've sold many tours to picturesque Scandinavia and the Baltic, but this is my first visit to these parts.

MIRANDA.

We're very glad that you're here.

BEN.

Thank you.

MIRANDA.

And what were you doing, Mr. Burnett?

JOE.

For the last two years I've been in jail—in one of General Franco's medieval dungeons.

MIRANDA.

You fought in Spain?

JOE.

Yes, Mrs. Valkonen.

MIRANDA.

Why, you're a hero, Mr. Burnett.

JOE.

No, Mrs. Valkonen. No hero. Just a bum. I went to Spain only because I was kicked out of Princeton.

DAVE.

What for?

JOE.

For throwing forward passes in chapel.

BEN.

All fliers are a little crazy. Now, you take Frank and me —we're sane. We're ambulance drivers. We're non-combatants, we hope. We'll have a good safe view of this country. And what I want to see most is some of those ski troops.

DAVE *looks at him, sharply.*

Will there be any of them around Viipuri?

JOE.

They're all up in the north, aren't they?

MIRANDA.

Yes. They're in the north.

Noticing JOE's *empty glass.*

Let me get you some more.

She takes JOE's *glass, rises and crosses to the serving table.*

DAVE.

Rising.

You won't see much action around Viipuri. The Mannerheim Line is just about as quiet as the Western Front.

MIRANDA.

Dave is always reassuring—at least when he's talking to me. But I think he's less optimistic when he's broadcasting the news.

DAVE.

That's only because I have to dramatize things for the radio audience. They like to be scared. In fact, every night, when I'm on the air, I have to remember that I'm in competition with a thriller program called "Renfrew of the Mounted."

FRANK.

I used to listen to that program. Renfrew always gets his man.

MIRANDA *looks at* FRANK, *surprised at his first contribution to the conversation.*

MIRANDA.

Did Dave say you lived in San Francisco?

FRANK.

Yes, Mrs. Valkonen.

MIRANDA.

And how long have you been away from home?

FRANK.

I came abroad just last summer. I was going to the Sorbonne in Paris.

MIRANDA.

Oh! You're a student.

FRANK.

Yes, I am. I had an exchange scholarship from my own school, Leland Stanford.

MIRANDA.

You must be brilliant! What sort of things were you studying?

FRANK.

Well—I particularly wanted to study French verse forms. I realize it sounds pretty ridiculous——

BEN.

The terrible truth is that Frank wants to be a poet.
     BEN *has to laugh at that.*

MIRANDA.

Now, really—I don't see anything to laugh at.

FRANK.

Perhaps you would if you could read any of my attempts.

MIRANDA.

I'd love to read some of your poetry. When I was a young girl, my greatest hero was Rupert Brooke. Maybe now that you're here—and have all this experience—maybe you'll write as he did. "Honour has come back, as a king to earth, And paid his subjects with a royal wage; and Nobleness walks in our ways again; and we have come into our heritage."

FRANK.

I'm afraid I could never write like Rupert Brooke, even if I were that good. He was always singing of the heroism of war.

MIRANDA.

Oh! And you see it as unheroic?

FRANK.

Yes, Mrs. Valkonen. I do.

BEN.

In addition to being a poet—Frank is also a rabid pacifist.

MIRANDA.

I'm glad to hear it. My husband is a pacifist, too. You must have a talk with him while you're driving to Viipuri.

FRANK.

I hope I have that privilege.

BEN

I've been a pacifist myself, in my time. I used to think, I'll never let my children grow up to get into this mass murder. But now I've got to the stage of figuring I ought to help put the murderers out of business *before* my children grow up and have to fight 'em themselves.

DAVE.

Have you got any children, Ben?

BEN.

No. It was all hypothetical.

MIRANDA.

But you came here, to Finland. You came through mine fields and submarines, didn't you?

FRANK.

Yes, we did.

MIRANDA.

What made you come through all that into this little war?

FRANK.

Because I'm a crazy fool, that's why.

MIRANDA.

That's interesting. How many crazy fools do you suppose there are in America?

DAVE.

I can name four hundred and seventy-three of my own acquaintance.

BEN.

The pioneers were fools. And as for that goof Columbus— why didn't *he* stay home and mind his own business?
He is crossing to help himself to another glass of eggnog.

DAVE.

Go easy on that punch, Ben. You've got to drive the ambulance.

BEN.

You can count on me, Dave.

MIRANDA.
To RUTKOWSKI.
Have you ever met any Americans before, Major?

RUTKOWSKI.

No, I'm sorry, I have not.

MIRANDA.

Then this will give you a faint idea.

RUTKOWSKI.

I am glad of the opportunity. I have often wondered what it could be like to be an American—to believe, even for a moment, that such things as peace and security are possible. You see, we have never been permitted such belief. For us, the sun rose each morning among our enemies and it set among our enemies. And now, it is high noon, and our enemies have joined together over our country— and we are gone.

DAVE.

It isn't always so completely delightful to be an American, Major. Sometimes even we have an uncomfortable feeling of insecurity. I imagine that Pontius Pilate didn't feel entirely at peace with himself. He knew that this was a good, just man, who didn't deserve death. He was against a crown of thorns on principle. But when they cried, "Crucify Him!" all Pilate could say was, "Bring me a basin of water, so that I can wash my hands of the whole matter."

> KAARLO *comes in, dressed in his uniform.* UNCLE WALDE-MAR *comes after him. All the guests rise.*

KAARLO.

No—please—don't get up. Gentlemen—this is my Uncle, Mr. Sederstrum.

UNCLE WALDEMAR.

How do you do?

All greet him. MIRANDA *is staring at* KAARLO *in his uniform. He looks at her, smiles lamely.*

KAARLO.

Now I'll have a glass of that eggnog. Then I suppose we should go?

RUTKOWSKI.

Looking at his watch.
I'm afraid so.

MIRANDA.

Bring a glass for Uncle Waldemar too, Dave.

BEN.

To think that I should be going to Viipuri in company with a winner of the Nobel Prize.

KAARLO.

I hope we don't get lost on the way. I have no sense of direction whatever. We'll rely on Major Rutkowski to guide us. The Major has been in the Mannerheim Line. Did he tell you about it?

This to MIRANDA, *as she pours his eggnog.*

MIRANDA.

No. He didn't.

KAARLO.

Oh—he says it's very dull there.

He lifts his glass.
Well, gentlemen, I beg leave to drink to you, our friends from the United States and from Poland.

They all move into a circle at the left.

DAVE.

Thank you, Doctor.

RUTKOWSKI.

And long life to the Republic of Finland!

ALL.

Hear, hear!

BEN.

And to you, Doctor.
They drink.

KAARLO.

Why, Miranda, it's good! Why don't we have this every
day?
> FRANK *goes to the piano and starts playing* "*Auld Lang
> Syne.*" *All sing. . . .* KAATRI *comes in at the right. She
> wears the Lotta uniform. She is very pale.*

MIRANDA.

Kaatri!
> *She goes quickly to* KAATRI, *who is looking wildly around
> the room at all the strangers.*

KAATRI.

Mrs. Valkonen—I had to see you——

MIRANDA.

Have you heard from Erik?

KAATRI.

No. But I must talk to you——

DAVE.

Come on, boys. Get your coats and hats on. We'll wait
outside, Mrs. Valkonen.

JOE.

Certainly.
> *They start to go out.*

MIRANDA.

You'll forgive me, Major Rutkowski. We'll be out in just a moment.

RUTKOWSKI.

Of course.
Rutkowski goes out at the right after DAVE, JOE, BEN *and* FRANK.
Now, Kaatri dear—what is it?

KAATRI.

I've written every day to Erik. I haven't heard from him since that first letter two weeks ago. I've got to see him, Mrs. Valkonen. Don't you think they could give him a little leave?

MIRANDA.

He'll surely have leave soon, dear. The Russians have to stop attacking some time. Isn't that so, Kaarlo?

KAARLO.

Of course it is. Erik's all right. In fact, he's probably enjoying himself. He likes that energetic life. Now—really—I must go. . . .
He starts to say good-bye to UNCLE WALDEMAR.

KAATRI.

No—please, Dr. Valkonen. There's something I have to ask you. I'm going to have a baby.

MIRANDA.
Rising.
Darling.
She takes her in her arms.

KAARLO.

Well! I'm very happy to hear it.

KAATRI.

I'm not happy. I don't want it! Dr. Valkonen! What can I do to stop it? Please tell me what I can do.

MIRANDA.

You're not ashamed, Kaatri? There's nothing for you to to be ashamed of.

KAATRI.

No—I'm not! But I don't want it. You've got to help me, Dr. Valkonen.

KAARLO.

Have you told your family of this?

KAATRI.

No. It wouldn't be easy for them to understand, as you do, about Erik and me.

MIRANDA.

Why don't you want to have a baby, Kaatri?

KAATRI.

I'm working. It would make me useless— just another person to be cared for——

MIRANDA.

That's not being useless.

KAATRI

It is now! What good would it be to bring a child into a world like this? He would have no country—no hope. *Please*, Dr. Valkonen. I'm sorry to be troubling you. But—just tell me some doctor that I can see.

KAARLO.

You will see Dr. Palm. Miranda—you know him.

MIRANDA.

Yes, Kaarlo.

KAARLO.

You take Kaatri to see him. Tell him that this is our daughter-in-law, and her baby will be our grandchild.
    KAATRI *looks at him, with terror.*
Yes, my dear, you are going to have that child.

KAATRI.
    Hysterical.
No—no! I won't have it!
    She tries desperately to break away from them.
I won't have a child born under a curse!

MIRANDA.

Quiet, dear. Please.
    She seats KAATRI *beside her.*

KAATRI.
    Making another frantic attempt to get away.
No! You won't help me. I'll find a doctor——

KAARLO.

Do as my wife tells you, Kaatri! You love Erik, and he loves you. You were willing to be married to him. You have taken responsibility. The highest responsibility! You are not going to evade it.

MIRANDA.

Kaatri—Kaatri!
    KAATRI *submits.* KAARLO *leans over her.*

KAARLO.

Whatever happens to our country, your child will not be born under a curse. It will be born to the greatest opportunity that any child has ever known, since the beginning of time. Remember that, and be brave. . . . Now —I can't keep them waiting. Good-bye, Uncle Waldemar. I'll be back soon.

UNCLE WALDEMAR.

Yes, Kaarlo. Good-bye.

They kiss. KAARLO *leans over and kisses* KAATRI'S *head. Then he takes* MIRANDA'S *hand. She rises, looks back, motions to* UNCLE WALDEMAR *to come to* KAATRI.

KAARLO.

Come on, darling.

They go out at the right. KAATRI *is crumpled up on the couch.* UNCLE WALDEMAR *goes over to her, sits down beside her, and takes her in his arms.*

UNCLE WALDEMAR.

Now—don't cry, Kaatri. Pay attention to what Dr. Valkonen told you. *He* knows what he is saying. If he tells you there is good hope, you can believe him.

CURTAIN

SCENE V

Dave Corween's room in the Hotel Kamp in Helsinki.

It is evening.

Upper right is a door leading to the corridor. At the left is a door leading to a bedroom.

The room is in pretty much of a mess. At the right, on a chair, is DAVE's *typewriter, with copy paper and carbon strewn about. At the left is a large table, on which is the same broadcasting apparatus seen in the first scene.*

DAVE *is at the microphone reading from a typescript before him.* GUS *is up-stage, left, with his earphones on.*

DAVE.

In an attempt to surround the main force of the Finnish army on the Karelian Isthmus, the Russians are now making determined attacks across Viipuri Bay. The

Mannerheim Line, supposedly impregnable bulwark of Finland's defense, has been shattered. The bombardment of these defenses, and of Viipuri itself, has now reached the terrible total of three hundred thousand shells a day. Looking at the ruination in Viipuri, I could not help thinking of the despairing prophecies made by H. G. Wells in *The Shape of Things to Come*. Here was the awful picture of the collapse of our Western civilization, the beginning of the Age of Frustration. Stores and factories, public libraries, museums, movie theatres—hospitals and schools and homes—all reduced to junk heaps. The Soviet Union is being generous in the expenditure of its ammunition, and extravagantly generous with the life blood of its men. Never again will these workers of the world arise! But in Moscow, the official propaganda bureau broadcasts constantly in Finnish, sending soothing encouragement to this beleaguered little country. Today I heard them say, and I quote, "The Red Army sends greetings to the workers of Finland. The Red Army does not destroy. That is why the workers in every country love the Red Army." And—perhaps, in the end —"love" will conquer all. . . . This is David Corween in Helsinki, returning you now to CBS in New York.

GUS *switches off the radio.* DAVE *turns to* JOE.
How was that, Joe? Do you think I'm holding my own against Renfrew of the Mounted?

JOE.
I think you're wasting your breath, Dave. Nobody's listening.

GUS.
I don't see how they can—with the complicated hook-up

we've got now. And if one of those bombs today had landed fifty yards farther west, there wouldn't be any broadcasting station here at all. Did you see those craters?

DAVE.

Yes.

GUS.

Boy! They must be dropping those two-ton bombs now, like they had in Spain.

DAVE.

Are you going to be flying around here now to protect us, Joe?

JOE.

I doubt it. I guess I'll get shipped right back to the lines.

GUS.

Well, I hope they don't keep us here until it's too late to get out. I'd hate to go through Warsaw again. I think I'll go down and see if I can get a cup of coffee. Where's the sugar?

DAVE.

Here.
He hands GUS *an envelope filled with sugar that has been lying on the couch.*

GUS.
To JOE.
See you later.

JOE.

Sure.
GUS *goes out.*

272

Say, Dave—when you were in Viipuri, did you see anything of Ben and Frank and Dr. Valkonen?

DAVE.

Yes. They got their hospitals established there and now they're working day and night to evacuate them. Ben and Frank don't seem to be having a very good time in this war.

JOE.

I guess they're in a tough spot now, with those attacks across Viipuri Bay.

DAVE.

Yes, I've got to go and see Mrs. Valkonen and try to think of something encouraging to say. Last week I was up in the north. I saw some of the ski troops in action.

JOE.

Did you see Mrs. Valkonen's son?

DAVE.

No. But I got an idea of what he must be going through. Poor kid. I remember the first time I came here he said that Finland wouldn't be in danger unless there was a counterrevolution in Russia. He had that much faith in them. Well—it seems that the counterrevolution has come.

JOE.

Something else has come. I saw something today that might interest you.

DAVE.

What is it?

JOE.

Maybe I oughtn't to be talking to the press.

273

DAVE.

Now listen, Joe—have another drink.

JOE.

Thanks.

He pours himself another drink.

DAVE.

You understand, Joe. Anything you tell me will be considered strictly confidential. I'll only try to pass it on the AP, the UP and the radio audience. But the censorship will stop me, so your secrets will be sacred.

JOE *drinks.*

JOE.

Well, they sent me out reconnoitering. I wanted to know what was the greatest point of Russian concentration. I had to fly very low. The weather was closing in and the ceiling was only seven or eight hundred feet, when I was coming back. I couldn't find the field I took off from. That's why I had to fly back here to make my report to the war office.

DAVE.

What did you report, Joe?

JOE.

I saw some staff cars coming up to the town that seemed to be general headquarters. I didn't know the name of the town, but I identified it for them on the map. I dived to give those cars a few bursts. They were full of staff officers, all right. But they weren't Russians. They were Nazis. It gave me a thrill. All this time, in fighting the Russians, I've felt just a little bit uncomfortable—you can imagine it, Dave, after my experience with the Loyalists. You know, I couldn't help saying, "God forgive them—for they know not what they do." If that's the right quotation.

DAVE.

It's good enough.

JOE.

But when I saw those Nazis—those arrogant bastards—and I could even see the looks on their faces—all I could think of was, "God forgive *me* if I miss this glorious opportunity." I let 'em have it. It was a beautiful sight to see 'em diving into the ditches, mussing their slick gray uniforms in the mud.

DAVE.

Did you get any of them?

JOE.

I'm afraid I'll never know. It was just then that the Russian planes came up. And I had to take my ship away from there.

DAVE.

I thought it was about time for the Nazis to be taking a hand in this war. No wonder the tide of battle has turned. I guess they've decided there has been enough of this nonsense of Finland's resistance. Probably they want the Russians to get busy somewhere else.

JOE *puts his glass down and stands up.*

JOE.

Is there any news from home?

DAVE.

Yes. . . . This has been the biggest season in the history

of Miami Beach. The University of Southern California won the national basketball championship. The Beaux Arts Ball was an outstanding success.

JOE crosses and looks into the bedroom at the left.

JOE.

Good! Say, Dave—can I have the use of that elegant bathtub of yours?

DAVE.

Certainly. There may be some hot water, and maybe not.

JOE.

How are you fixed for a clean shirt and underwear and socks?

JOE goes into the bedroom.

DAVE.

I guess Gus and I can fit you out between us.

DAVE follows JOE out. There is a knock at the door at the right.

Come in!

MIRANDA comes in. Her face is pale. She comes in quietly, closing the door behind her. DAVE calls from off left.

I'll be right out.

MIRANDA looks around the room, then sits down. After a moment DAVE comes back, and is startled to see her.

Mrs. Valkonen!

He closes the bedroom door behind him.

MIRANDA.

Hello, Dave. I hope I'm not disturbing you. Mr. Shuman told me I might come up—I met him in the lobby.

DAVE.

Of course, Mrs. Valkonen. I apologize for the mess here.
. . . Would you like anything to drink?

MIRANDA.

No, thank you. I came to ask you for some help, Dave.

DAVE.

Anything that I can do——

MIRANDA.

I want to get my daughter-in-law out of this country.

DAVE.

Your daughter-in-law?
  He sits down, near her.

MIRANDA.

Yes. You've met her—Kaatri. She was married a few
days ago to my son, Erik. They were married in the hospital, before he died.

DAVE.

Oh—I'm terribly sorry.

MIRANDA.

I know you're sorry, Dave. . . . Kaatri is going to have a
baby. . . . She's very ill. I've made all the arrangements
to get her to Norway, and then to New York. But she
has to leave right away. I need some American money,
Dave. Could you lend me fifty dollars? It will be paid back.

DAVE.

Will that be enough?

MIRANDA.

Oh, yes—that will be plenty. And—
  She opens her handbag and takes out a sheet of paper.

—here is the name and address of my aunt in Boston. When you get back to America, just write to her and tell her where to send the money.

DAVE *takes the paper and puts it down on the table. He takes out his wallet.*

You see—the Finnish money is worth very little in foreign exchange now. By the time Kaatri arrives in New York, it might be completely worthless. That's why I had to have dollars. If it's inconvenient for you—I'm sure I can get it somewhere else—so please don't hesitate to——

DAVE.

It's perfectly convenient, and I'm very much flattered that you came to me.

He gives her the fifty dollars.

MIRANDA.

Thank you. We had an awful time persuading Kaatri to go. We never could have persuaded her if she weren't too ill to resist. She's strong—but there are limits.

She puts the money in her handbag.

DAVE.

I wish you were going with her.

MIRANDA.

I wish I could. I should like to be present at the birth of my grandchild. Poor Kaatri. She'll have a bad time of it, all alone there. . . . Perhaps she'll have a son, and he'll grow up a nice, respectable New Englander and go to Harvard and wonder why he has an odd name like Valkonen. . . . Erik wasn't very badly wounded. He might have pulled through if he hadn't been in such a state

278

of terrible exhaustion. It was a lucky thing that we learned where he was and got to him. I sent word to Kaarlo. I don't know where he is—somewhere around Viipuri.

She looks at DAVE.

They're getting closer, aren't they, Dave?

DAVE.

Yes.

MIRANDA *rises.*

MIRANDA.

I'm very grateful for that loan. I hope you will come to see Uncle Waldemar and me. We're always there.

DAVE.

Thank you, Mrs. Valkonen. I—I wish to God you'd let me really *do* something.

MIRANDA.

But you've done a lot, Dave. That fifty dollars——

DAVE.

It's not much satisfaction to know that fifty dollars is the best I can do.

MIRANDA.

It's all I want, Dave. All I can use. I was desperately anxious to get Kaatri out of the country. You can understand why. It means one little link with the future. It gives us the illusion of survival—and perhaps it isn't just an illusion. . . . Good-bye, Dave.

DAVE.

Good-bye.

MIRANDA *goes out.*

CURTAIN

279

SCENE VI

Classroom in a little country schoolhouse in eastern Finland. It is afternoon of a gloomy day, a few days after the preceding scene.

This schoolhouse is new and clean, designed in the the most modern style. Huge, opaque glass windows would admit plenty of soft sunshine if there were any today.

At the center upstage is a dais. Before it is a row of pupil's desks. The size of these desks indicates that this is a classroom for little children of nine or ten. There is a blackboard with arithmetical problems. On the walls are tacked rows of sketches done by the pupils. Around the room on the walls are painted, in decorative, colored Finnish script, the first ten lines of the Kalevala. (Of course, half of these lines are on the walls which we do not see.) On the window sills, little plants are sprouting in pots.

There is a door at the extreme left, leading to the little enclosed porch, and a door at the extreme right, leading to another schoolroom.

At one of the pupils' desks, the right one, GOSDEN *is sitting solemnly playing solitaire with an old, dirty pack. He is a mild, tired Englishman, about forty years old. He wears the uniform of an infantry soldier. His rifle lies on the desk before him. There is a scuffle at the door, left.* GOSDEN *leaps to his feet, picks up his rifle and aims it at the door.* BEN GICHNER *and* FRANK OLMSTEAD *come in. Both carry large haversacks. Both are very cold.*

GOSDEN.

Who are you?

BEN and FRANK *raise their arms immediately.*

BEN.

Friends! We're not Russians and we're not armed.

GOSDEN.

Lowering his rifle.
Glad to see you. Sorry but I'm a bit jumpy these days.

BEN.

That's all right, pal.

GOSDEN.

Americans, eh!

BEN.

That's right. What are you—English?

GOSDEN.

Yes. The name is Gosden. I don't rightly know what my rank is in this army, but I call myself "Sergeant."

BEN.

Crossing and shaking hands with GOSDEN.
Glad to know you, Sergeant. My name is Ben Gichner—
this is Frank Olmstead.

FRANK.

Glad to know you.
Frank sits at the desk at the left.

GOSDEN.

Thank you. It's a pleasure to have your company. I was
getting the wind up, all alone here.
Sees their uniforms.
You chaps in the Medical Corps?

BEN.

Yes. Ambulance drivers. Only—we've lost our ambulance
—it's frozen stiff as a goat in a snowdrift. When the
Russians occupy this territory they'll come into possession of a Buick.

GOSDEN.

You wouldn't have much use for it here. There haven't
been many wounded since we retreated from the Mannerheim Line. Only dead and missing.
FRANK *rests his head on his arms.*

FRANK.

How far are the Russians from here?

GOSDEN.

I wish I knew. They've probably occupied those islands
out there in Viipuri Bay. Maybe they've already reached
this shore. All I can say is the last time I saw them they
were coming in this direction, driving us across the ice.

I've been retreating across the ice for days. I've felt like
a bloody Eskimo.

He looks about the room.

Nice little schoolhouse, this.

He reaches in his pocket.

Like a bit of chocolate?

FRANK.

No, thanks.

BEN.

Sitting up.

I'll have some.

GOSDEN.

Tossing him some candy.

It's good for energy.

BEN.

Thanks, pal.

FRANK.

How long have you been in this war?

GOSDEN.

I joined up in London, just after Christmas.

FRANK.

Why? What did you want to come here for?

GOSDEN.

Smiles.

Are you trying to trap me into making any remarks about
fighting for freedom and democracy?

FRANK.

Wearily.

No.

GOSDEN.

Because I had enough of *that* muck when I fought in the last war!

FRANK.

I'm just interested to know why *any*body volunteered.

GOSDEN.

Well, you might say that my case is no different from any of the others. I came because I was bored, fed up. My wife and two little children were sent to Cornwall in the evacuation. Then I lost my job. I was working in the furniture department at Harrod's—and who wants to buy furniture in wartime? I couldn't join up with our own army—too old. All I could do was walk the streets looking at nothing. There was no news to read in the papers—except about heroic little Finland. On Christmas, I felt I couldn't stick it out any longer. So—I thought— why not have a go at heroic little Finland? And here I am. Where I shall be tomorrow, I really couldn't say.

> RUTKOWSKI *comes in from the left, followed by* KAARLO, *who wears a Red Cross arm band on his uniform. All the men rise to attention.*

RUTKOWSKI.

At ease! Are there any more men here?

GOSDEN.

No, sir. Only me. I was with Captain Vertti's company, but we got separated. I didn't know just where to go next, sir, so I stopped here for a bit of a rest.

RUTKOWSKI.

Has there been much shelling here?

GOSDEN.

I've heard plenty of heavies, overhead, but none dropping here, sir. There's also been a lot of Bolshie planes, flying low—looking the situation over, I expect.

RUTKOWSKI.

They're probably shelling the railroad line between Viipuri and Helsinki. Trying to cut off all possibilities of re-inforcement. I'm going out to find if there is anyone in command here.

KAARLO is greatly interested in the schoolroom. He crosses to the right.

KAARLO.

This schoolhouse would do well for a field ambulance station.

BEN and FRANK have sat down.

GOSDEN.

Still standing.

Begging your pardon, sir. You couldn't find a more exposed place.

RUTKOWSKI.

Yes—you might say that this *is* Finland—small clean—and exposed.

With a slight shrug.

I shall be back presently, Doctor.

He goes out at the left.

KAARLO.

We'll be waiting, Major.

To GOSDEN.

I'm Dr. Valkonen. How do you do?

Somewhat to GOSDEN'S *surprise,* KAARLO *extends his hand. They shake.*

GOSDEN.

Thank you, sir. My name is Gosden.

KAARLO.

I gather that things here are a bit disorganized.

GOSDEN.

And no wonder, sir. It's a miracle that there's any sign of an army left—the way they've been pushing us.

GOSDEN *sits.* KAARLO *crosses to the dais and looks at the blackboard.*

KAARLO.

You know—they must have left this school very quickly —right in the midst of an arithmetic lesson. Look— there's a multiplication problem that was never finished. The pupils were probably delighted but—

Pointing to the sketches.

—they evidently had to leave without knowing which picture won first prize.

BEN.

How old would the kids be in a school like this?

KAARLO.

From seven to twelve, I should judge. It's just a little country school. I wish you could see it when the children are here. The boys are on that side, the girls there. When the teacher comes in, the boys all rise and bow stiffly. The girls make their little curtsies. Maybe in their hearts they loathe the teacher—but they're always very polite. And all very full of moral preachments. Oh, yes. . . . You see that inscription all around the walls? That's from the

Kalevala—the epic poem of Finland. It had its beginnings in the songs of our minstrels a thousand years ago. Your poet, Longfellow, knew the Kalevala and used its rhythm in Hiawatha.

He looks up, and starts to recite, at first with a sort of tender amusement, and then with increasing solemnity. His eyes travel about the room as he follows the inscription.

> "Let us clasp our hands together,
> Let us interlock our fingers;
> Let us sing a cheerful measure,
> Let us use our best endeavors
> While our dear ones hearken to us,
> And our loved ones are instructed,
> While the young are standing round us,
> Of the rising generation,
> Let them learn the words of magic,
> And recall our songs and legends."

He is quiet for a moment, looking toward the right. Then he turns to the others.

Every Finnish child learns about the Kalevala—just as Americans learn those words about Life, Liberty and the Pursuit of Happiness.

FRANK.
Earnestly.
Dr. Valkonen——

KAARLO.
Yes, Frank?

FRANK.
I've wanted to ask you a question——

KAARLO.

Yes?

FRANK.

About your book—

FRANK *pulls a paper-covered book, badly dog-eared, from his jacket pocket.*

KAARLO.

You've been carrying that around with you?

FRANK.

Yes. I bought it in Viipuri when we first went there.

BEN.

Frank is more worried about your book, Doctor, than he is about the Russians.

FRANK.

He opens the book to the last page.

There's a lot of it I don't understand, but what I wanted to ask you about most is the very end.

KAARLO.

What is it at the end?

FRANK.

Reads.

"How long, O Lord, before we shall hear the sound of the Seventh Angel of the Apocalypse? Have you forgotten the promise of St. John? 'And they shall see his face, and his name shall be in their foreheads. And there shall be no night there and they need no candle, neither light of the sun; for the Lord giveth them light; and they shall reign forever and ever.' How long, O Lord, before we shall be given to see the true revelation?"

FRANK *closes the book and looks at* KAARLO.

288

Why did you conclude a scientific work with Biblical words—and what do you mean by the true revelation?

KAARLO.

Simply.

It's the revealing to us of ourselves—of what we are—and what we may be.

Smiles.

Of course—we can all use the Book of Revelation to substantiate our own theories. It's an eternally effective device. I have heard evangelist charlatans quote it to prove that if you do not accept their nonsense and pay for it, you will most surely burn in hell. But there is something profound in those words I quoted. That unknown Jewish mystic who wrote that—somehow, unconsciously, he knew that man will find the true name of God in his own forehead, in the mysteries of his own mind. "And there shall be no night there." That is the basis of all the work I have done.

FRANK.

And how do you feel about that work now, Dr. Valkonen?

KAARLO.

I think I've learned a great deal in the last few months. Research work in the field! I never dreamed I would have such a vast laboratory, with so many specimens.

BEN.

Have you arrived at any new conclusions, Doctor?

KAARLO.

Not conclusions, I'm afraid. Just—somewhat stronger suspicions. It is wonderful to see what men are capable of—what courage—what endurance—what utter lack of selfishness. And what a tragedy that these heroic qualities can be tested only by disease. That's what all this is, you know—disease. All of this—reasonless war—aimless revolution—it's a psychological epidemic.

He rises. It is as though he were lecturing to a class. Scientists had seen it coming, for a long time, long before 1914, even. But we had no conception of its extent. And now the very belief of men that they can insulate themselves against it is in itself a sign of lunacy. The germs of that disease travel on the air waves. The only defenses are still here—behind the forehead. . . .

He pauses and smiles, looking particularly at GOSDEN. I apologize, gentlemen, for carrying on a conversation which must be extremely boring to you.

GOSDEN.

I'm an ignorant man, sir. I haven't read this book. I didn't even know I was in the presence of anyone who had written a book. But—from what you've said—I have a feeling it's all hopeless. I shouldn't care to die believing *that.*

KAARLO.

Then you won't die believing it's hopeless. That's the point, my friend. You have lived in faith—the light is in you—and it is the light which gives the strength that defeats death. It's only the fearful—the unbelieving— those who have sold themselves to the murderers and the liars—they are the only ones who can really die.

FRANK.

But how can you deny that the light is going out—it's going fast—everywhere?

KAARLO.

With a growing sense of excitement.

It is just beginning to burn with a healthy flame. I know this, because I have seen it. I have seen it in all kinds of men, of all races, and all varieties of faith. They are coming to consciousness. Look at all the millions of men now under arms, and all those that are fearful that arms may be thrust upon them. Are there any illusions of glory among any of them? None whatever! Isn't that progress?

BEN.

Far be it from me to argue, Doctor—but I can't see the difference whether men go to war because of illusions of glory, or just in a spirit of grim resignation.

KAARLO.

There is all the difference. Because those illusions, when shattered, leave men hollow. When men lose their illusions, they say, "Oh, what's the use? What have we got to live for?" They are devitalized by the conviction of futility. But grim resignation, as you call it, that makes a man say, "This is an evil job—but I have to do it." And when men say that, they are already beginning to ask, "But *why* do I have to do it? *Why* must this evil go on forever?" And when men start asking questions, they are not satisfied until they find the answers. That is consciousness. And for the first time in history, consciousness is not just the privilege of a few secluded philosophers. It is free for all. For the first time, individual men are fighting to know themselves. . . . Forgive me, gentlemen. I forget myself. I think I am lecturing at the Medical Institute. But—

He pauses to listen to the guns.

—the Russians are only a short distance away. This may be my last lecture. So—please permit me to finish. . . . Listen! What you hear now—this terrible sound that fills the earth—it is the death rattle. One may say easily and dramatically that it is the death rattle of civilization. But —I choose to believe differently. I believe it is the long deferred death rattle of the primordial beast. We have within ourselves the power to conquer bestiality, not with our muscles and our swords, but with the power of the light that is in our minds. What a thrilling challenge this is to all Science! To play its part in the ultimate triumph of evolution. To help speed the day when man becomes genuinely human, instead of the synthetic creature—part bogus angel, part actual brute—that he has imagined himself in the dark past——

The sound of an approaching motorcycle is heard.

Is that an aeroplane?

All the men listen, tensely.

GOSDEN.

No. It's a motorbike.

The sound stops.

Just a despatch rider, I expect. Maybe it's orders.

JOE BURNETT *comes in from the left.*

JOE.

Hello, Ben. Hello, Frank. Hello. Dr. Valkonen.

FRANK.

Joe!

BEN.

Where did *you* drop from?

JOE.

I saw Major Rutkowski up the road. He said you were in here.

KAARLO.

Mr. Burnett! I am delighted to see you. Are you flying on this front now?

JOE.

I was—up till half an hour ago. I was shot down. First time that ever happened to me. I just managed to make a landing behind our lines. I got a motorcycle and I'm going back to headquarters to see if they have any more planes.

GOSDEN.

Were you scouting the Russian lines?

JOE.

Yes.

GOSDEN.

How do things look?

JOE.

Not too good. They're bringing up everything.

BEN.

Have you been in Helsinki lately, Joe?

JOE.

Yes. I was there a few days ago.

BEN.

Is Dave Corween still on the job?

JOE.

Yes. He's still telling bedtime stories.

KAARLO.

And I hope you called at my house, Mr. Burnett? Did you see my wife?

JOE.

No—I didn't.

He braces himself and crosses to KAARLO.

I—I don't know how to say it, Dr. Valkonen—although God knows I've said it so many times before—but—I want you to know that you have my sympathy.

KAARLO.

Your sympathy?

KAARLO *looks at him with such intense questioning that* JOE *gulps.*

Why do I have your sympathy, Mr. Burnett?

JOE.

You don't know about your son?

KAARLO.

No.

He looks levelly at JOE.

He's dead?

JOE.

Yes.

KAARLO.

Killed in action?

JOE.

I believe he died in hospital, of wounds.

KAARLO.

When was this?

JOE.

I don't quite know. I heard of it only from Dave. He had seen Mrs. Valkonen.

KAARLO.

Is—my wife well?

JOE.

Yes, Doctor. She told Dave that she had been with your son in the hospital. He was married there, to Miss Alquist, before he died. His wife has gone to America. . . . I—I didn't know, Doctor, that I should be the bearer of this news—

His voice trails off.

GOSDEN.

Rising, and speaking with great diffidence.
I should like, sir, to be permitted to put in my word of sympathy, too.

BEN.

And mine also, Doctor.

FRANK.

Rising.
Wouldn't you like us to get out of here, Dr. Valkonen?

KAARLO.

No, no. Thank you. And thank you for telling me, Mr. Burnett. I imagine my wife has written me all this, but we have moved about so much that there have been no letters in weeks. I'm sorry you had to undergo this embarrassment.

RUTKOWSKI *comes in. He carries a cartridge belt with a revolver in a holster.*

RUTKOWSKI.

I found the commanding officer. The Russians have occupied all the islands around Uuras. They're bringing tanks over the ice, and they're going to attack in force here. The Finns are forming up to drive them back. They need more men. They seem to be organizing the defense very well. But they have no reserves. They need more men. There's no point in trying to organize a field ambulance station here, Doctor. I brought this revolver and belt for you. It was salvaged from some officer who was killed. There are rifles for you men to use.

He hands the belt and holster to KAARLO, *who takes out the revolver and stares at it.*

FRANK.

We're to fight?

RUTKOWSKI.

There's no compulsion if you don't wish to go.

JOE.

Quietly.

I'll be glad to go, Major.

BEN.

So will I.

RUTKOWSKI.

To JOE.

Not you, Lieutenant. If there are any planes left, we need them in the air. You will report back to headquarters at Sakkijaarvi.

JOE.

Resigned.

Very good, sir.

KAARLO.

We must go now? At once?

RUTKOWSKI.

We may as well wait here for a little while. There will be plenty of warning when the attack starts.

KAARLO.

Then—I would like to write a letter.
He puts the revolver and belt down on the desk.
Perhaps you will take it with you, Mr. Burnett? There must be some way that they could send it on to Helsinki.

JOE.

I'll do everything I possibly can, Dr. Valkonen.

KAARLO.

To RUTKOWSKI.
If I'm not finished when you're ready to go, just call me.

RUTKOWSKI.

I will, Doctor.
KAARLO *goes out at the right, taking his fountain pen from his pocket.*
Have any of you gentlemen a cigarette?
BEN *hands him one.*
Thank you. . . . I supose Dr. Valkonen wants to write his valedictory.

JOE.

It isn't that, Major. I just gave him the news that his son was killed.

RUTKOWSKI.

Oh—when I came in—I saw his face—but I didn't know the explanation.

He lights his cigarette, being careful to mask the flame with his greatcoat.

FRANK.

With sudden vehemence.

Do you know that Dr. Valkonen believes in the teachings of Christ? He believes in them as if they were scientific facts, which can yet be proved. He says so in his book. He says you can't resist evil by building Maginot Lines and big navies. The true defenses of man are *in* man, himself. . . . So now—there's nothing left for that great thinker to do but take a gun and go up there and shoot.

He has crossed above the desks and looks at the revolver.

BEN.

And how about you, Frank? Are you going up? What does the old conscience say?

FRANK.

What the hell do you think it says? How could I ever live with myself again if I didn't go? That's what happens when you expose yourself to this. Oh, God—how many times have I taken an oath that if the United States were ever again duped into going to war, I'll be a conscientious objector! Let them put me in Leavenworth. I'd rather be there. I'd consider it takes more courage to be there than in the front line. But—here's the choice—given to me now—and I haven't got the guts to say, "No—I won't fight."

He has crossed to the left and sits down on the floor beside JOE. RUTKOWSKI *is sitting on the center desk. The others are seated at the other desks.*

BEN.

Why don't you put all that into a poem, Frank?

FRANK.

All right, Ben—go ahead and kid me.

BEN.

I don't feel in a position to kid you, Frank. I've had a few necessary changes of heart myself. Once I lost a good job because they decided I was a Red. Yes. I've spent hours arguing that the Soviet Union is the greatest sociological advance in history—the greatest force for peace on earth today. . . . Now—go ahead and kid *me!*

RUTKOWSKI.
   Bitterly.
Nobody is responsible for his opinions now. There *are* no opinions on anything.

GOSDEN.
   To RUTKOWSKI.
How do our positions look in the line, sir?

RUTKOWSKI.
Fairly well placed.

GOSDEN.
Do you think we would have any chance of holding them?

RUTKOWSKI.
   With no emotion.
No—I don't think so.

BEN.
   With a nervous laugh.
I take it, Major—you feel we're all condemned to death?

299

RUTKOWSKI.

Yes.

BEN *stands up. He is whistling.*

BEN.

I can't help agreeing with you, Frank. It seems a silly way to end your life.

JOE.

Any way is silly. A cousin of mine was killed—he and his girl both—driving home from a debutante party at the Ritz in New York. He was a little tight, and he didn't notice the Dead End sign—and—phft!—right into the East River!

FRANK.

And is that any reason why we should fight—and die?

GOSDEN.

To FRANK.

Every one of us can find plenty of reasons for *not* fighting, and they're the best reasons in the world. But—the time comes when you've bloody well got to fight—and you might just as well go cheerfully.

FRANK.

Rising to his knees.

Cheerful! What are you, anyway? Are you so stupid you can't even *think?* You said you have a wife and two little children in England. Aren't you giving any thought to them now?

GOSDEN.

In a choked voice.

I'll have to ask you not to mention them. My people know what I'm doing—and why.

FRANK.

Sinking back on his heels.

Excuse me.

RUTKOWSKI.

Looking off toward the left.

Poor Dr. Valkonen. He is a philosopher. He is also, for some strange reason, an optimist. He will be better dead.

BEN.

Why do you say that, Major?

RUTKOWSKI.

Perhaps it is only because I am Polish.

He looks levelly at FRANK.

You asked this gentleman to give a thought to his wife and children in England. He can think of them happily. My wife—my baby—my father—and mother—are in Warsaw—or they were there, when the Nazis came. My wife is twenty-four years old. She is very beautiful. She is the most beautiful person I have ever known. And I have read in Cardinal Hlond's report, that he has sent to the Pope—I have read that the good-looking women and the girls in Poland have been sent into Germany to be whores.

He rises quickly and raps at the door at the right. He turns to the others.

Well!

GOSDEN.

In a desperate effort to change the subject.

I wish I'd thought to write a line myself. I *did* think of it —but I didn't know what to say. I wish I'd written to my missus to tell her I'm going up the line in good company.

KAARLO comes in from the right. He is sealing the envelope. BEN slaps GOSDEN on the back.

KAARLO.

Here you are, Mr. Burnett.

JOE crosses and gets the letter from KAARLO.

JOE.

I'm sure it will be delivered safely.

He shakes hands with KAARLO, and salutes RUTKOWSKI, who returns the salute.

KAARLO.

Thank you so much.

JOE.

Good-bye, sir.

GOSDEN picks up his coat and rifle. All are now making preparations to go. KAARLO goes to the desk to get the belt and revolver and put them on.

GOSDEN.

To JOE.

Best of luck, mate.

JOE.

Same to you.

GOSDEN goes out. JOE is about to go.

BEN.

Joe, if you ever get back, I wish you'd send a word to my mother, Mrs. Bessie Gichner—Cincinnati. You can get her address at the American Express Company's main office in New York. They all know me there.

JOE.

As BEN goes out.

I'll remember that, Ben . . .
He starts out.
If I get back——

FRANK.

Hey, Joe—wait a minute. I've got a message, too!
JOE *and* FRANK *have gone out on this.* RUTKOWSKI *has been watching* KAARLO *with silent sympathy as he puts on the belt.*

RUTKOWSKI.

Forgive me, Dr. Valkonen. I hadn't known of the great loss you have suffered.

KAARLO.

Thank you. I had been expecting that news for a long time. I was prepared for it. My son had a good character —part Finnish, part American. He was not afraid.
He starts to go. RUTKOWSKI *is by the door at the left.*

RUTKOWSKI.

Doctor, I think you had better take off that Red Cross arm band.
RUTKOWSKI *goes. It is now so dark that* KAARLO *is a silhouette as he rips off the Red Cross arm band. He goes out. The sound of the guns increases.*

CURTAIN

SCENE VII

The Valkonens' living room. The only noticeable difference in the room is that all the autographed photographs have been removed from their frames.

UNCLE WALDEMAR is at a window, looking out. It is a beautiful, sunny day.

After a moment, DAVE and JOE come in from the dining room. UNCLE WALDEMAR turns quickly.

UNCLE WALDEMAR.

I was enjoying the beautiful day.

DAVE.

It *is* beautiful. It's beginning to feel almost like spring.

UNCLE WALDEMAR.

Did you have a nice lunch?

DAVE.

Wonderful, thank you.

UNCLE WALDEMAR.

I'll go help Miranda clear the dishes.

DAVE.

We begged to be allowed to help, but were ordered out of the kitchen.

UNCLE WALDEMAR.

Of course.
   He gives them a courtly bow.
You are guests.
   He goes out. DAVE *offers* JOE *a cigarette.*

DAVE.

An incredible display of stoicism.

JOE.

God—I didn't know what to say. I never know what to say. Anything you can think of sounds so lame.

DAVE.

You didn't need to say anything, Joe. She's lost everybody that she loves—and now she's in terrible danger of losing her own life. But it's a matter of principle that neither she nor anyone else must ever admit that there are certain undertones of tragedy in the situation. After all the centuries, New England is still New England. You might even go so far as to say that it's still England. Keeping a stiff upper lip.

JOE.

How long do you figure it will take the Russians to get here?

DAVE.

I don't know. But I suspect it won't be long. Berlin has

given out orders that this little incident must end—and if the Russians don't hurry, there are going to be some serious tantrums in the Wilhelmstrasse.

JOE.

This city might hold out for a long time, like Madrid.

DAVE.

I hope not. Because if it comes to a siege, you'll see German battleships out there, doing their bit in the bombardment. I wouldn't like to be here when that happens. I saw them at Danzig when they were battering Westerplatte. I could see the Nazis, watching their own barrage. They were deriving a sexual thrill from that display of devastating power.

JOE.

What happens to you when you get caught in a captured city?

DAVE.

I know how to wave my little red passport. I can say "I'm an American journalist" in all languages. In Nanking, I had to say it in Japanese. Oh—I get pushed around a bit—but I always live to broadcast the final hours of another gallant little republic. . . . But what about you, Joe? Have you got a plane?

JOE.

I don't know. I may be in the army now. It would be pretty humiliating to end my career in the god-damned infantry.

DAVE.

Looking toward the kitchen.

306

That's what Dr. Valkonen did.

JOE *also glances toward the kitchen.*

JOE.

Listen, Dave—can't you get Mrs. Valkonen out of this—
and the old man, too?

DAVE.

I've tried—but they won't leave. They're going to wait
here for whatever comes, the Russians, or the Nazis, or
both. They've even planned how they'll burn the house
down. That's required by Finnish tradition. It's like the
scorched earth in China. Mrs. Valkonen wants to stay
here and die, just as her husband did. She doesn't care
what happens.

JOE.

It's a pity.

DAVE.

That's just what it is, Joe. A wholesale pity. Three
months ago, the Soviet troops marched in. They had brass
bands and truck-loads of propaganda with them. They
thought it would be a grand parade through Finland, like
May Day in the Red Square. So now—several hundred
thousand men have been killed—millions of lives have
been ruined. The cause of revolution all over the world
has been set back incalculably. The Soviet Union has been
reduced from the status of a great power to that of a
great fraud. And the Nazis have won another bloodless
victory.

MIRANDA *and* UNCLE WALDEMAR *come in from the kitchen.*
MIRANDA *wears an apron, but her dress is, as always,
very feminine and chic.* DAVE *and* JOE *rise.*

MIRANDA.

Well—we've washed all the dishes and put them away neatly, and now Uncle Waldemar and I haven't a thing to do until supper. Sit down, Dave—Mr. Burnett.

JOE.

I'm sorry, Mrs. Valkonen. I have to go and report for duty, whatever it is.

MIRANDA.

Oh—I'm sorry. But thank you so much for coming, and bringing the letter, and telling me all about that little schoolhouse.

JOE.

I—I'm glad I could get here. You've been very kind to me. I can tell you that—I won't ever forget you, or Dr. Valkonen. . . . Good-bye, Mr. Sederstrum.
He shakes hands with UNCLE WALDEMAR.
Good-bye, Dave—I'll probably be seeing you.
He shakes hands with DAVE.

DAVE.

Yes, Joe—good-bye.

JOE.

And if you get home before I do, don't forget those messages for Ben's and Frank's families.

DAVE.

I won't, Joe.

MIRANDA.

I wish you the very best of luck, Mr. Burnett.

JOE.

You needn't worry about me, Mrs. Valkonen. The beautiful part of my life is that it's so utterly worthless nobody bothers to deprive me of it. Good-bye.

He goes out at the right.

MIRANDA.

I hope he comes through all right. He's the only one left of those young men who went to Viipuri with Kaarlo . . . I suppose you'll be going soon, Dave?

DAVE.

I'm not sure, Mrs. Valkonen. There's some talk of their sending me to Stockholm. They want to investigate those peace rumors.

MIRANDA.

Do you think there might be peace before the Russians get here to Helsinki?

DAVE.

I hope so.

UNCLE WALDEMAR.

In a completely matter-of-fact tone.

It doesn't make much difference. Either the war continues and we suffer the fate of Poland, or peace comes, as it did at Munich, and we become another Czechoslovakia. In any case, we live only at the mercy of the enemy.

MIRANDA.

You'll have a great book to write about all this—won't you, Dave? Your own personal history.

DAVE.

I'm afraid that words will fail me, Mrs. Valkonen. Just as they've failed the whole human race.

MIRANDA.

I'd like to read your book, Dave.

DAVE.

He looks at her.

What are you going to do, Mrs. Valkonen? Are you—are you planning just to sit here and wait for them?

MIRANDA.

Oh no, we have our plans all made. Get out the guns, Uncle Waldemar.

UNCLE WALDEMAR *goes out at the right.*

DAVE.

Guns?

MIRANDA.

We got them at the hospital. They'd been discarded by wounded soldiers. Uncle Waldemar and I have been practicing—not shooting, of course; but just learning how to work them. When this war started, Dave—when the Russians first attacked us—the President said we would fight —even the women, and the old people, and the children would fight. We have no children here—only that one in Boston, who is unborn. But Uncle Waldemar and I are here.

UNCLE WALDEMAR *returns with two army rifles and some cartridge belts.*

When we see them coming from the shore down there, we'll light the fire. It's all ready, down in the cellar. Then we'll go out into the garden, behind the stone wall, with the guns and ammunition.

She takes one of the rifles and a clip of ammunition.

You see—you put the clip in like this—then you shove the bolt.

She shoves it with a snap.
After each shot, you twist it and pull it back, to throw
out the empty shell. Like this . . .
*She demonstrates, manipulating the bolt. The shells fly
out.*
What do you think of that, Dave?
She looks up at the 1812 portrait.
Great-grandfather Eustis thinks it's fine!
*There is something maniacal in this statement. She
puts the gun against the wall and picks up a parcel
from the piano.*
I hate to add to your burdens as a carrier of bad news,
Dave. But—I have a package here, that I want you to
take, and also a letter from Kaarlo—the one he wrote in
the schoolhouse before he was killed. The package con-
tains Kaarlo's signed pictures of Freud and Pavlov and
Carrel and the Mayos. He was very proud of those pictures. There's also the Nobel gold medal. I want you to
take the package and the letter and give them to Kaatri,
to keep for her child. You have that address in Boston—
my aunt, who is going to pay you back the fifty dollars
I borrowed?

DAVE.
Yes. I have the address.

MIRANDA.
Looking at the letter.
Kaarlo had just heard from me about Erik's death. He
wanted to comfort me, in his curious way. Do you mind
if I read you the letter?

DAVE.
Please do, Mrs. Valkonen.

MIRANDA.

Reading.

"In this time of our own grief it is not easy to summon up the philosophy which has been formed from long study of the sufferings of others. But I must do it, and you must help me." You see—he wanted to make me feel that I'm stronger—wiser. "I have often read the words which Pericles spoke over the bodies of the dead, in the dark hour when the light of Athenian democracy was being extinguished by the Spartans. He told the mourning people that he could not give them any of the old words which tell how fair and noble it is to die in battle. Those empty words were old, even then, twenty-four centuries ago. But he urged them to find revival in the memory of the commonwealth which they together had achieved; and he promised them that the story of their commonwealth would never die, but would live on, far away, woven into the fabric of other men's lives. I believe that these words can be said now of our own dead, and our own commonwealth. I have always believed in the mystic truth of the resurrection. The great leaders of the mind and the spirit—Socrates, Christ, Lincoln—were all done to death that the full measure of their contribution to human experience might never be lost. Now—the death of our son is only a fragment in the death of our country. But Erik and the others who give their lives are also giving to mankind a symbol—a little symbol, to be sure, but a clear one—of man's unconquerable aspiration to dignity and freedom and purity in the sight of God. When I made that radio speech"—you remember? . . . "I quoted from St. Paul. I repeat those words to you now, darling: 'We glory in tribulations; knowing that tribulation worketh patience; and patience, experience; and experience, hope.' There are men here from all different countries. Fine men. Those Americans who were at our house on New Year's Day—and that nice Polish officer, Major Rutkowski—they are all here. They are waiting for me now, so I must close this, with all my love.''

She folds the letter and hands it to DAVE.

There it is, Dave. Take good care of it.

DAVE.

I shall, Mrs. Valkonen. But it may be a long time before I can deliver it.

MIRANDA.

It will be a long time before my grandchild learns to read.

DAVE.

After a moment's silence.

I—I have to be going now . . .

He goes quickly to UNCLE WALDEMAR.

Good-bye, Mr. Sederstrum.

UNCLE WALDEMAR.

Shaking hands with DAVE.

Good bye, Mr. Corween.

MIRANDA.

You'll surely let us know if you're going to Stockholm?

DAVE.

Oh, yes, Mrs. Valkonen.

MIRANDA.

We'll miss you very much, Dave. You've really become part of our life here in Helsinki.

MIRANDA *and* DAVE *have gone out on that.* UNCLE WALDE-

MAR *looks after them, then he sits down at the piano. Still looking toward the door, he starts to play the Finnish folk song heard at the end of the first scene. After a moment,* MIRANDA *returns. She goes to the couch, and sits down where she had sat beside* KAARLO. *She listens to* UNCLE WALDEMAR's *playing. She looks to the left, where* ERIK *had been, and to the right, where* KAARLO *had been. She leans backward, wearily, and looks at nothing.* UNCLE WALDEMAR *goes on playing the tinkly little tune. There is a kind of peace in this Finnish-American house.*

CURTAIN

THE END

INDEX

315

70 71 72 73 10 9 8 7 6 5 4 3 2 1